FamilyCircle®

Hometown COOKING

Volume 1

Meredith® Books
Des Moines, Iowa

Family Circle® *Hometown Cooking*
Editor: Lois White
Contributing Editor: Shelli McConnell
Contributing Writer: Lisa Kingsley
Associate Design Director: Todd Emerson Hanson
Contributing Designer: The Design Office of Jerry J. Rank
Copy Chief: Terri Fredrickson
Copy Editor: Kevin Cox
Publishing Operations Manager: Karen Schirm
Senior Editor, Asset and Information Management: Phillip Morgan
Edit and Design Production Coordinator: Mary Lee Gavin
Art and Editorial Sourcing Coordinator: Jackie Swartz
Book Production Managers: Pam Kvitne, Marjorie J. Schenkelberg, Mark Weaver
Imaging Center Operator: Rich Van Winkle
Contributing Copy Editor: Carol DeMasters
Contributing Proofreaders: Stacie Gaylor, Elise Marton, Donna Segal
Contributing Indexer: Elizabeth T. Parsons

Meredith® **Books**
Editor in Chief: Gregory H. Kayko
Executive Director, Design: Matt Strelecki
Managing Editor: Amy Tincher-Durik
Executive Editor: Jennifer Darling
Senior Editor/Group Manager: Jan Miller
Senior Associate Design Director: Ken Carlson

Executive Director, Marketing and New Business: Kevin Kacere
Director, Marketing and Publicity: Amy Nichols
Executive Director, Sales: Ken Zagor
Director, Operations: George A. Susral
Director, Production: Douglas M. Johnston
Business Director: Janice Croat

Senior Vice President: Karla Jeffries
Vice President and General Manager: Douglas J. Guendel

Family Circle® **Magazine**
Editor in Chief: Linda Fears
Editorial Director: Michael Lafavore
Creative Director: Karmen Lizzul
Food Director: Regina Ragone, R.D.
Senior Food Editor: Julie Miltenberger
Associate Food Editor: Michael Tyrrell
Assistant Food Editor: Cindy Heller
Editorial Assistant: Katie Kemple
Test Kitchen Associate: Althea Needham

Meredith Publishing Group
President: Jack Griffin
President, Better Homes and Gardens®: Andy Sareyan
Vice President, Corporate Solutions: Michael Brownstein
Vice President, Manufacturing: Bruce Heston
Vice President, Consumer Marketing: David Ball
Consumer Product Marketing Director: Steve Swanson
Consumer Product Marketing Manager: Wendy Merical
Business Director: Jim Leonard

Meredith Corporation
Chairman of the Board: William T. Kerr
President and Chief Executive Officer: Stephen M. Lacy

In Memoriam: E.T. Meredith III (1933–2003)

Pictured on the front cover:
Creamy Caramel-Pecan Rolls (page 38)

Cover photography:
Photographer: Pete Krumhardt
Food Stylist: Charles Worthington
Prop Stylist: Brenda Peterson

Enjoy our best-loved recipes from hometown America!

There's some really great food you just can't get in a restaurant. It's the homey, soul-satisfying food you've enjoyed at church potlucks, neighborhood picnics, local fairs and festivals—and at your best friend's kitchen table.

The *Family Circle® Hometown Cooking* annual is a coast-to-coast collection of just those kinds of recipes. We gathered prizewinning and most-requested recipes from the country's best cooks—from community cookbooks, cooking contests and tried-and-true regional favorites.

Among the more than 200 recipes are dishes for starting the day, throwing a party, getting a weeknight dinner on the table in less than 30 minutes—and, of course, lots of yummy things to satisfy your sweet tooth.

Along the way, you'll enjoy meeting some of the people who contributed these recipes—folks like you—who love cooking and celebrating with friends and family.

The *Family Circle Hometown Cooking* annual offers recipes you'll make again and again—and pass on to others countless times.

–the editors

Contents

Chapter 1

Get Started

Appetizers

Pick from these party-perfect appetizers and drinks to make your next gathering a memorable one. A variety of classics and twists on tradition mean there is something for every taste.

Tricolor Tapenade

Pam's Best Brie

When people are lucky enough to be invited to a summer cookout at Pam and Don Verhille's cabin that overlooks the Mississippi River, they might indulge in this warm, gooey appetizer while they sip a glass of wine and watch barges navigate the river and bald eagles swoop across the sky. "Everyone loves to come to the river," Pam says.

PREP: 15 minutes
CHILL: 1 to 5 hours
BAKE: toasts at 350° about 5 minutes per side; Brie for 12 to 15 minutes
MAKES: 20 servings

- ¾ jar (7 to 8 ounces) oil-packed dried tomatoes
- ⅓ cup finely chopped shallots or onion
- 4 teaspoons finely chopped garlic
- 1 tablespoon chopped fresh basil leaves or 1 teaspoon dried basil
- ½ cup chopped fresh parsley leaves
- ⅛ teaspoon black pepper
- 2 rounds (15 ounces each) Brie, with rind
  Baguette-style French bread slices, for serving
  Fresh basil leaves, for garnish

1. Drain oil from tomatoes; reserve 3 tablespoons. Chop tomatoes to make ½ cup.

2. In large skillet, cook shallots in 2 tablespoons reserved oil until tender. Stir in garlic and cook 1 minute. Add tomatoes and basil and cook for 2 minutes. Remove from heat. Stir in parsley and pepper.

3. Line baking sheet with foil; top with Brie rounds. Brush with remaining oil. Spread tomato mixture on top. Cover and refrigerate for 1 to 5 hours.

4. Heat oven to 350°. Arrange bread slices on another baking sheet. Bake at 350° until light brown, about 5 minutes per side.

5. Bake Brie, uncovered, on center oven shelf for 12 to 15 minutes or just until edges melt. Lift by foil to plate; trim foil. Garnish with additional basil. Serve with toasted bread slices.

Per serving: 162 cal., 13 g total fat (8 g sat.), 43 mg chol., 289 mg sodium, 3 g carbo., 1 g fiber, 9 g pro.

Pam's Best Brie

Shrimp-Stuffed Mini Cream Puffs

Shrimp-Stuffed Mini Cream Puffs

Sara Drummond is so passionate about gardening that she drives 96 miles round trip from her home to Pine Mountain, Georgia, once or twice a month to "play in the dirt" as a volunteer at Callaway Gardens. She made this elegant recipe for her daughter's wedding reception and contributed the recipe to the cookbook *Flavors of the Gardens*.

PREP: 30 minutes
BAKE: at 400° about 18 minutes
COOL: 10 minutes
MAKES: 24 cream puffs

Cream Puffs:
1	cup water
½	cup (1 stick) butter
½	teaspoon salt
1	cup all-purpose flour
4	eggs

Shrimp Filling:
1	pound medium or small shrimp, shelled and deveined
1	package (8 ounces) cream cheese, softened
1	teaspoon grated onion or ½ teaspoon onion powder
½	teaspoon dry mustard
¼	teaspoon salt
¼	teaspoon Worcestershire sauce
⅛	teaspoon black pepper
3	hard-cooked eggs, finely chopped
½	cup finely chopped celery

1. Cream Puffs: Heat oven to 400°. Grease baking sheets. In medium-size saucepan, combine water, butter and ½ teaspoon salt. Bring to a boil. Add flour all at once, stirring vigorously. Cook and stir until mixture forms ball. Remove from heat. Cool for 10 minutes. Add eggs, one at a time, beating well with wooden spoon after each addition. Drop dough from teaspoon onto prepared baking sheets, forming mounds 1 inch in diameter and spacing mounds about 1½ inches apart. Bake at 400° about 18 minutes or until golden. Remove to rack; let cool.

2. Shrimp Filling: In saucepan, cook shrimp in small amount of lightly salted boiling water for 1 to 2 minutes or until shrimp turn pink. Drain. Rinse with cold water; drain and pat dry. Finely chop shrimp. In large bowl, mix cream cheese, onion, dry mustard, ¼ teaspoon salt, Worcestershire sauce and pepper. Stir in shrimp, egg and celery.

3. To serve, cut tops from puffs; remove soft dough. Spoon in filling. Replace tops.

Per cream puff: 128 cal., 8 g total fat (6 g sat.), 110 mg chol., 178 mg sodium, 4 g carbo., 0 g fiber, 6 g pro.

Fresh Summer Salsa

You might expect that the cookbook from the Junior Service League of Brownsville, Texas, would have some Tex-Mex touches. Connie Fischer, who gets the credit and applause for getting the cookbook produced, developed this colorful salsa that has all the hallmarks of close-to-the-border cooking: fresh tomatillos, fiery serrano chiles and fresh lime.

PREP: 35 minutes
CHILL: 1 to 24 hours
MAKES: 24 (2-tablespoon) servings

¼	cup finely chopped red onion
¼	cup ice water
2	tablespoons white-wine vinegar
4	tomatillos (about 4 ounces total)
¾	cup finely chopped yellow cherry tomatoes
2	plum tomatoes, finely chopped (about ⅔ cup)
1½	teaspoons chopped fresh cilantro leaves
1	serrano chile, seeded and finely chopped*
1	teaspoon fresh lime juice
	Salt and black pepper
	Tortilla chips, for serving

1. In medium-size nonmetal bowl, combine onion, ice water and vinegar. Let stand for 30 minutes.

2. Meanwhile, remove and discard thin, papery husks from tomatillos. Rinse and finely chop (there should be about ¾ cup).

3. Drain onion mixture. Stir in tomatillos, cherry and plum tomatoes, cilantro, chile and lime juice. Season to taste with salt and pepper. Cover and refrigerate for 1 to 24 hours. Serve with tortilla chips.

*Note: Serranos and other hot chiles contain oils that can burn your skin and eyes. Avoid direct contact with them as much as possible. When working with hot chiles, wear plastic or rubber gloves. If your bare hands do touch chiles, wash your hands well with soap and warm water.

Per serving (salsa only): 5 cal., 0 g total fat (0 g sat. fat), 0 mg chol., 14 mg sodium, 1 g carbo., 0 g fiber, 0 g pro.

Fresh Summer Salsa

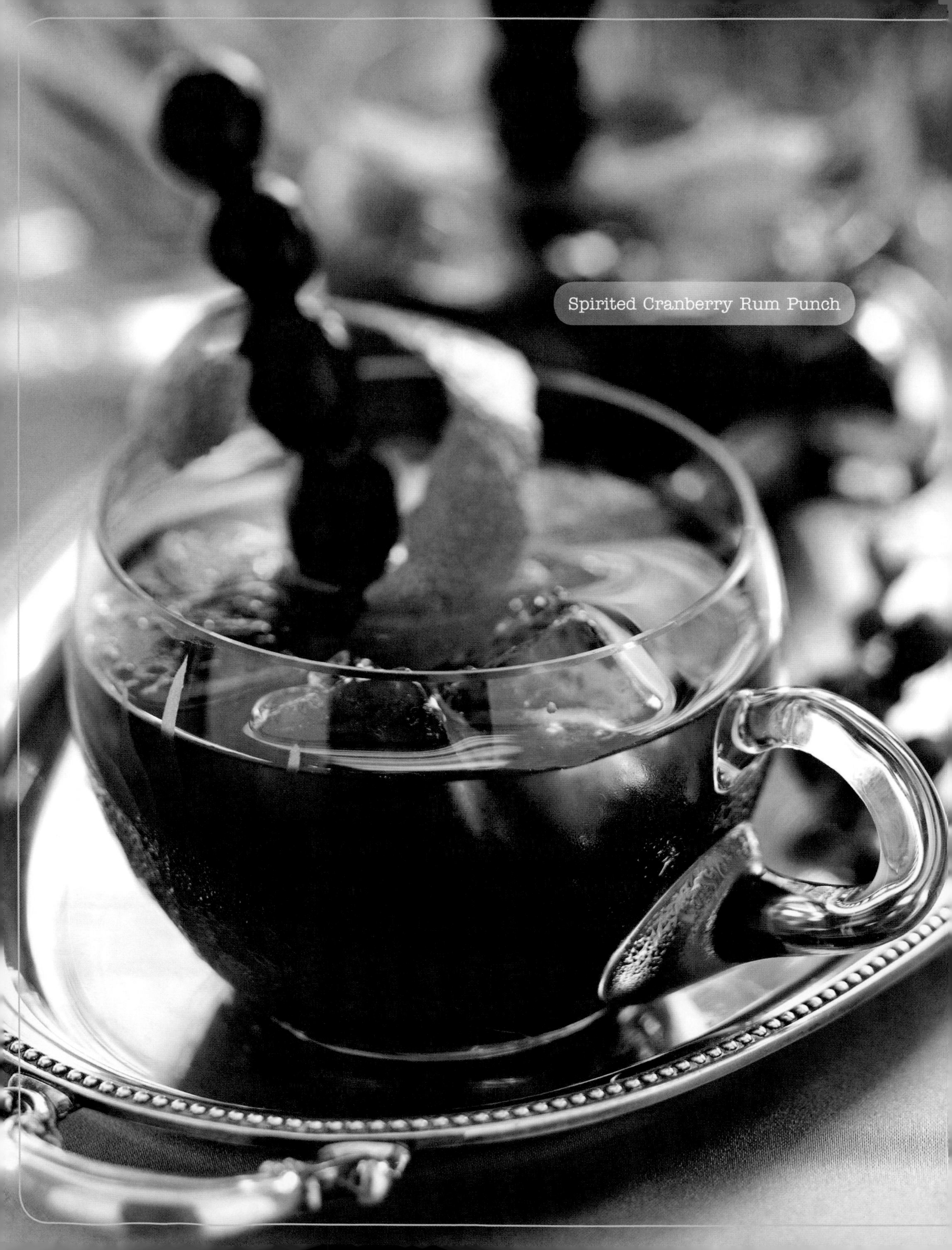

Spirited Cranberry Rum Punch

Spirited Cranberry Rum Punch

Generally, spirits that are mixed with other ingredients don't have to be of premium quality, so don't feel that you have to splurge on the best bottle you can buy to enjoy this fun and fuss-free holiday punch.

PREP: 5 minutes
MAKES: 3 to 4 servings

1	cup cranberry juice or any flavor cranberry juice blend
½	to ⅔ cup dark rum
	Ice cubes

1. In small pitcher, combine cranberry juice and rum. Pour over ice in short cocktail glasses.

Per serving: 112 cal., 0 g total fat (0 g sat.), 0 mg chol., 2 mg sodium, 12 g carbo., 0 g fiber, 0 g pro.

Holiday Honey Punch

Use a mild-flavored honey, such as clover, to make this festive punch so that the taste of the honey doesn't overwhelm the rest of the flavors.

PREP: 15 minutes
CHILL: 2 to 24 hours
MAKES: 18 servings

2	cups boiling water
¾	cup honey
4	cups cranberry juice
2	cups orange juice
½	to 1 cup lemon juice
1	bottle (1 liter) ginger ale, chilled

1. In large heatproof pitcher or bowl, combine boiling water and honey. Set aside to cool.

2. Add cranberry, orange and lemon juices to honey mixture. Cover and refrigerate for 2 to 24 hours.

3. To serve, transfer punch mixture to large punch bowl. Gradually pour ginger ale down the side of the bowl. Stir gently to combine.

Per serving: 108 cal., 0 g total fat (0 g sat.), 0 mg chol., 7 mg sodium, 28 g carbo., 0 g fiber, 0 g pro.

Citrus-Raspberry Cooler

Light, bubbly and ever-so-feminine, this is the perfect punch for a bridal or baby shower. Be sure to use plain raspberry-flavored sparkling water—not sweetened water, or even water labeled "sugar free." Either one will make your punch taste too sweet.

PREP: 15 minutes
CHILL: 2 to 24 hours
MAKES: 12 servings

2	**cups water**
⅓	**cup sugar**
5	**raspberry-flavored herbal tea bags**
1	**can (6 ounces) frozen orange juice concentrate, thawed**
2	**bottles (1 liter each) red raspberry-flavored sparkling water, chilled**
	Ice cubes
	Lemon slices, for garnish (optional)

1. In small saucepan, combine water and sugar. Bring to a boil, stirring to dissolve sugar. Remove from heat.

2. Add tea bags. Let steep for 5 minutes. Discard tea bags. Transfer mixture to medium-size bowl. Stir in juice concentrate. Refrigerate for 2 to 24 hours.

3. To serve, pour chilled tea mixture into large punch bowl. Slowly pour in sparkling water; stir gently. Serve in ice-filled glasses with lemon slices, if desired.

Per serving: 38 cal., 0 g total fat (0 g sat.), 0 mg chol., 32 mg sodium, 10 g carbo., 0 g fiber, 0 g pro.

Watermelon Cooler

On the hottest summer day, this gorgeous, sparkling refresher will cool you from the inside out.

PREP: 15 minutes
CHILL: 2 to 24 hours
MAKES: 10 servings

Watermelon Ice Cubes:
  Watermelon, cut into 1-inch cubes
Beverage:
5   cups seeded and cubed watermelon (about 3½ pounds)
⅓   cup raspberry or cherry syrup
1   bottle (1 liter) carbonated water, chilled
    Raspberry or cherry syrup (optional)

1. Watermelon Ice Cubes: In 15×10×1-inch baking pan, place melon cubes in a single layer. Freeze for 1 to 2 hours or until firm. If storing longer than 4 hours, transfer cubes to a plastic freezer bag or freezer container and keep frozen until ready to use.

2. Beverage: In blender or food processor, combine 5 cups cubed watermelon and ⅓ cup syrup. Cover and process until smooth. Press mixture through fine mesh sieve into medium-size bowl; discard pulp. Cover and refrigerate mixture for 2 to 24 hours.

3. To serve, add Watermelon Ice Cubes to ten 12-ounce glasses. Pour enough watermelon mixture into glasses to fill halfway. Add enough carbonated water to fill glasses. If desired, sweeten individual servings with additional syrup; stir to dissolve syrup.

Per serving: 44 cal., 0 g total fat (0 g sat.), 0 mg chol., 22 mg sodium, 11 g carbo., 0 g fiber, 0 g pro.

Vodka Lemon Slush

Here's a slush for grown-ups! Cold and citrusy, this spirited sparkler is great to have stashed in the freezer, ready for a steamy, hot day.

PREP: 10 minutes
FREEZE: 8 to 24 hours
MAKES: 20 servings

2   cans (6 ounces each) frozen lemonade concentrate, thawed
2   cans (6 ounces each) frozen limeade concentrate, thawed
1   can (6 ounces) frozen orange juice concentrate, thawed
3½   cups water
2   cups vodka
1   cup sugar
     Carbonated water or lemon-lime carbonated beverage, chilled

1. In extra-large nonmetal container, mix juice concentrates, water, vodka and sugar. Cover and freeze mixture for 8 to 24 hours.

2. To form a slush, scrape a large spoon across the top of frozen mixture. For each serving, place ½ cup slush in an 8-ounce glass. Fill each glass with carbonated water.

Per serving: 172 cal., 0 g total fat (0 g sat.), 0 mg chol., 27 mg sodium, 29 g carbo., 0 g fiber, 0 g pro.

Salsa and Cheese Dip

Queso fresco is a soft, crumbly Mexican cheese.

PREP: 30 minutes
BAKE: chips at 425° for 8 to 10 minutes
CHILL: 2 to 3 hours
MAKES: 12 (2-tablespoon) servings

Dip:
¼	cup fresh flat-leaf parsley leaves
2	tablespoons fresh cilantro leaves
1	tablespoon fresh oregano leaves
1	tablespoon pistachio nuts
1	scallion (white portion, only), cut up
1	carton (8 ounces) sour cream
½	cup crumbled queso fresco or farmer cheese (2 ounces)
3	tablespoons green salsa
	Few drops hot-pepper sauce

Chips:
8	(6-inch) corn tortillas
2	teaspoons garlic-pepper blend
½	teaspoon coarse salt

1. Dip: In food processor, combine parsley, cilantro, oregano, pistachios and scallion. Process until finely chopped. In small bowl, combine sour cream, queso fresco, salsa and hot-pepper sauce. Stir in herb mixture. Cover and refrigerate for 2 to 3 hours or until serving time.

2. Chips: Heat oven to 425°. Lightly coat tortillas on both sides with nonstick cooking spray. Sprinkle tortillas on both sides with pepper blend and salt. Make two stacks of 4 tortillas each. Cut each stack into six wedges. Place in a single layer on two baking sheets. Bake one sheet at a time at 425° for 8 to 10 minutes or until light brown and crisp. Cool on baking sheets. Serve dip with chips.

Per serving: 105 cal., 6 g total fat (3 g sat.), 10 mg chol., 160 mg sodium, 10 g carbo., 2 g fiber, 3 g pro.

Cowboy Caviar

This light and chunky salsa will disappear like lightning from the buffet table. Use a hot and spicy salsa if you like your food with some heat.

PREP: 15 minutes
CHILL: 3 to 24 hours
MAKES: about 27 (2-tablespoon) servings

½	package (16 ounces) frozen black-eyed peas (about 1⅔ cups), or 1 can (15 ounces) black-eyed peas, rinsed and drained
1	cup finely chopped scallions or onion
¾	cup finely chopped sweet red or green pepper
1	can (4 ounces) diced green chiles, drained
½	cup bottled salsa
½	cup Italian salad dressing
1	teaspoon bottled chopped garlic
⅛	teaspoon black pepper
	Few dashes hot-pepper sauce
	Tortilla chips or large corn chips, for serving

1. Cook frozen black-eyed peas following package directions. Drain and rinse in colander.

2. In large nonmetal bowl, combine scallions, sweet pepper, chiles, salsa, salad dressing, garlic, black pepper and hot-pepper sauce. Add black-eyed peas, stirring gently to combine. Cover and refrigerate for 3 to 24 hours.

3. Serve with tortilla chips for dipping.

Per serving (caviar only): 35 cal., 2 g total fat (0 g sat.), 0 mg chol., 55 mg sodium, 3 g carbo., 1 g fiber, 1 g pro.

Beer Cheese Spread

This terrific dip is perfect for armchair football parties—but it travels well to tailgates too. Make a double batch for a big crowd; leftovers will keep for weeks in the refrigerator.

PREP: 10 minutes
STAND: 30 minutes
MAKES: 12 (2-tablespoon) servings

2	**cups finely shredded Cheddar cheese (8 ounces)**
¼	**cup beer**
3	**tablespoons tomato paste**
2	**teaspoons Worcestershire sauce**
¼	**teaspoon garlic powder**
	Toasted pita chips, assorted crackers or tortilla chips, for serving

1. In medium-size bowl, let cheese stand at room temperature for 30 minutes.

2. Add beer, tomato paste, Worcestershire sauce and garlic powder to cheese. With an electric mixer on medium speed, beat until well mixed, scraping sides of bowl. Serve immediately or cover and refrigerate until serving time.

3. To serve, transfer dip to serving bowl. Serve with toasted pita chips, crackers or tortilla chips.

Per serving (spread only): 82 cal., 6 g total fat (4 g sat.), 20 mg chol., 160 mg sodium, 2 g carbo., 0 g fiber, 4 g pro.

Buffalo Chicken Dip

You get all the great flavors of classic Buffalo hot wings in this warm and creamy dip (but your hands will stay a lot neater in eating it).

PREP: 10 minutes
COOK: 10 minutes
MAKES: 20 (2-tablespoon) servings

- 2   large boneless, skinless chicken breast halves (1 pound total)
- 6   tablespoons hot sauce (such as Frank's)
- 1   package (8 ounces) cream cheese, cut into 1-inch chunks
- ½   cup ranch or blue cheese dressing
- ½   cup shredded Cheddar cheese (2 ounces)
  - Assorted crackers, for serving

1. Place chicken breasts in medium-size skillet and add enough water to cover. Bring to a boil over high heat. Reduce heat to medium, cover and poach for 6 to 7 minutes or until internal temperature reaches 170° on an instant-read meat thermometer. Remove chicken to a plate to cool. Shred with two forks. Discard poaching liquid.

2. In the same skillet, combine shredded chicken and hot sauce; heat through. Add cream cheese and dressing; heat until well blended. Add ¼ cup of the shredded cheese; stir until melted.

3. To serve, transfer to crock; sprinkle remaining shredded cheese on top. Serve warm (reheat in microwave if needed) with crackers.

Per serving (dip only): 103 cal., 8 g total fat (4 g sat.), 30 mg chol., 292 mg sodium, 1 g carbo., 0 g fiber, 7 g pro.

Reuben Dip

This hot, bubbly dip has all the great flavors and textures of the classic sandwich that bears its name, but it's a lot easier to eat!

PREP: 10 minutes
BAKE: at 350° for 30 minutes
MAKES: 32 (2-tablespoon) servings

- ½   pound diced corned beef
- 1   package (8 ounces) cream cheese, softened
- 1   cup shredded Swiss cheese (4 ounces)
- 1   cup sauerkraut, drained well
- ½   cup sour cream
- 1   tablespoon ketchup
- 2   teaspoons spicy brown mustard
  - Rye crackers or rye bread, for serving

1. Heat oven to 350°. Grease 1-quart casserole dish. Set aside.

2. In medium-size bowl, mix corned beef, cream cheese, Swiss cheese, sauerkraut, sour cream, ketchup and mustard. Spoon into prepared dish.

3. Bake at 350° about 30 minutes or until hot and bubbly. Serve warm with rye crackers or bread.

Per serving (dip only): 65 cal., 5 g total fat (3 g sat.), 19 mg chol., 169 mg sodium, 1 g carbo., 0 g fiber, 3 g pro.

Bruschetta with Tomatoes and Basil

Bruschetta with Tomatoes and Basil

Get a step out of the way: Toast bread, cool it and store slices in an airtight container at room temperature for up to 24 hours.

PREP: 20 minutes
BROIL: 3 minutes
MAKES: 8 servings

Topping:
- 2 medium-size red or yellow tomatoes, chopped
- 1 small sweet yellow pepper, chopped
- ½ cup lightly packed fresh sweet basil leaves, stacked, rolled, and thinly sliced
- 1 clove garlic, finely chopped
- 1 tablespoon extra-virgin olive oil
- ¼ teaspoon sea salt or salt

Bruschetta:
- 2 tablespoons extra-virgin olive oil
- ½ teaspoon black pepper
- 1 loaf (8 ounces) baguette-style French bread, ends trimmed and sliced ½ inch thick

1. Topping: In medium-size bowl, combine tomatoes, yellow pepper, basil, garlic, 1 tablespoon olive oil and salt.

2. Bruschetta: Heat broiler. In small bowl, combine 2 tablespoons olive oil and pepper. Brush one side of 16 bread slices with olive oil mixture (reserve any remaining bread for another use). Place brushed slices on an ungreased baking sheet, oiled side up. Broil 3 to 4 inches from heat for 2 to 3 minutes or until light brown.

3. To serve, top toasts with tomato mixture and arrange on platter. Serve within 45 minutes.

Per serving: 133 cal., 6 g total fat (1 g sat.), 0 mg chol., 225 mg sodium, 17 g carbo., 1 g fiber, 3 g pro.

Italian-Style Wontons

If you wish, serve these Asia-meets-Europe wontons with warm marinara sauce.

PREP: 30 minutes
COOK: in 365° oil for 1 to 2½ minutes per batch
MAKES: 24 wontons

- ½ cup finely shredded mozzarella cheese (2 ounces)
- ¼ cup chopped fresh basil leaves
- ¼ cup chopped walnuts
- 3 tablespoons oil-packed dried tomatoes, drained and finely chopped
- 2 tablespoons finely chopped pitted ripe olives
- 1 scallion, trimmed and thinly sliced
- 24 wonton wrappers
  Vegetable oil or shortening for frying

1. Heat oven to 300°. In bowl, combine cheese, basil, walnuts, tomatoes, olives and scallion.

2. For each wonton, place one wonton wrapper on flat surface with a corner facing you. Spoon a rounded teaspoon of filling just below center of wrapper. Fold bottom point over filling and tuck it under filling. Roll wrapper once to cover filling, leaving about 1 inch unrolled at top of wrapper. Moisten right corner with water. Grasp right and left corners and bring them toward you below the filling. Overlap corners and press firmly to seal.

3. In large, heavy saucepan or deep-fat fryer, heat 2 inches of oil to 365°. Fry wontons, a few at a time, for 1 to 2½ minutes or until golden brown. Drain on paper towels. Keep warm in 300° oven while frying remainder.

Per wonton: 55 cal., 4 g total fat (1 g sat.), 2 mg chol., 41 mg sodium, 4 g carbo., 0 g fiber, 1 g pro.

Glazed Ham Balls and Smokies

When you're in need of a substantial and satisfying appetizer, this twist on classic cocktail meatballs and wieners fits the bill. The sauce is sparked with cranberries and ground ham adds a sweet and smoky touch to the meatballs.

PREP: 30 minutes
BAKE: ham balls at 350° for 15 minutes
COOK: 2 to 3 hours on high-heat setting
MAKES: 25 servings

Ham Balls:
- 1   egg, lightly beaten
- ½   cup graham cracker crumbs
- ¼   cup finely chopped onion
- 2   tablespoons chopped dried cranberries
- 2   tablespoons milk
-      Dash ground cloves
- ½   pound ground cooked ham
- ½   pound lean ground pork

Cranberry Glaze:
- 1   can (16 ounces) jellied cranberry sauce
- 1   bottle (12 ounces) chili sauce
- 1   tablespoon vinegar
- ½   teaspoon dry mustard

Smokies:
- 1   package (16 ounces) small cooked smoked sausage links

1. Ham Balls: Heat oven to 350°. In large bowl, combine egg, graham cracker crumbs, onion, cranberries, milk and cloves. Add ham and pork; mix well. Shape mixture into 50 balls.

2. Lightly coat a 15×10×1-inch baking pan with nonstick cooking spray. Arrange ham balls in a single layer on prepared pan. Bake at 350° for 15 minutes. Drain well.

3. Cranberry Glaze: In medium-size saucepan, combine cranberry sauce, chili sauce, vinegar and dry mustard. Cook and stir over medium heat until cranberry sauce is melted.

4. In 3½- to 5-quart slow cooker, combine ham balls and sausage links. Pour cranberry glaze over mixture in cooker. Cover slow cooker; cook on high-heat setting for 2 to 3 hours. Serve immediately or keep warm on low-heat setting for up to 2 hours. Serve ham balls and sausage with wooden toothpicks.

Per serving: 138 cal., 7 g total fat (2 g sat.), 29 mg chol., 524 mg sodium, 13 g carbo., 1 g fiber, 6 g pro.

Mandarin Apricot Chicken Wings

Tricolor Tapenade

Lining the baking pan with foil before loading it up with saucy chicken wings makes cleanup a cinch.

PREP: 15 minutes
BAKE: at 400° about 25 minutes
MAKES: 24 servings

2	pounds chicken wing drumettes (about 24)*
⅔	cup sweet and sour sauce
½	cup chopped dried apricots
⅓	cup hoisin sauce
¼	cup soy sauce
2	tablespoons honey
2	cloves garlic, finely chopped
¼	teaspoon ground ginger
¼	teaspoon five-spice powder
1	tablespoon sesame seeds, toasted

1. Heat oven to 400°. Arrange drumettes in single layer on foil-lined baking pan or roasting pan. Bake at 400° for 20 minutes.

2. In small saucepan, combine sweet and sour sauce, apricots, hoisin sauce, soy sauce, honey, garlic, ginger and five-spice powder. Bring to a boil; reduce heat. Simmer, uncovered, for 5 minutes. Remove from heat.

3. Brush about ¼ cup of sauce mixture over drumettes. Sprinkle with sesame seeds. Bake about 5 minutes more or until drumettes are no longer pink in center. Transfer drumettes to a platter and serve with remaining sauce.

*Note: If you can't find drumettes, use 12 chicken wings. Cut off and discard wing tips or reserve for making broth. Cut each wing into 2 sections (drumettes).

Per serving: 86 cal., 5 g total fat (1 g sat.), 29 mg chol., 274 mg sodium, 7 g carbo., 0 g fiber, 5 g pro.

This Mediterranean-style spread, flavored with rich-tasting imported Greek kalamata olives, is also delicious spread on sandwiches or tossed with hot cooked pasta. Pictured on page 7.

PREP: 20 minutes
MAKES: 24 servings

¼	cup pitted ripe olives, such as kalamata
¼	cup pimiento-stuffed green olives
¼	cup purchased roasted red peppers
1	teaspoon chopped fresh oregano leaves
1	teaspoon olive oil
¼	teaspoon black pepper
12	baguette-style French bread slices, toasted,* or melba toast rounds
6	ounces soft goat cheese (chèvre)

1. In food processor, pulse olives, red pepper, oregano, olive oil and black pepper until coarsely chopped.

2. To serve, spread toasted bread slices with goat cheese; top with olive mixture.

*Note: To toast bread slices, heat oven to 350°. Arrange bread slices on baking sheet. Bake at 350° until lightly browned, about 5 minutes per side.

Per serving: 65 cal., 4 g total fat (2 g sat.), 7 mg chol., 171 mg sodium, 4 g carbo., 1 g fiber, 3 g pro.

Old City BBQ Shrimp

Old City BBQ Shrimp

Turn this spicy starter into a simple summer meal: Serve it with a crisp green salad, corn on the cob and French bread.

PREP: 25 minutes
BAKE: at 350° about 15 minutes
MAKES: 12 servings

1½	pounds medium-size shrimp in shells
2	tablespoons butter, melted
1	tablespoon Worcestershire sauce
1	tablespoon lemon juice
1	clove garlic, finely chopped
¾	teaspoon seafood seasoning (such as Old Bay)
¾	teaspoon Cajun seasoning
¾	teaspoon hot-pepper sauce
¼	teaspoon black pepper

1. Heat oven to 350°. Lightly grease 13×9×2-inch baking pan. Shell and devein shrimp, leaving tails intact. Rinse shrimp; pat dry with paper towels. Place shrimp on prepared baking pan.

2. In small bowl, combine melted butter, Worcestershire sauce, lemon juice, garlic, seafood seasoning, Cajun seasoning, hot-pepper sauce and pepper. Pour mixture over shrimp on pan. Toss to coat. Arrange shrimp in a single layer on pan.

3. Bake at 350° about 15 minutes or until shrimp turns opaque. Spoon shrimp into serving dish. Pour cooking liquid over shrimp. Serve immediately.

Per serving: 53 cal., 3 g total fat (1 g sat.), 52 mg chol., 135 mg sodium, 1 g carbo., 0 g fiber, 6 g pro.

Gouda Pecan Poppers

Gouda (GOO-dah) is a semifirm Dutch cheese that has an assertive but mild flavor that goes terrifically with nuts. Here it's pecans, but these pop-in-your-mouth morsels would be delicious with almonds or hazelnuts too.

PREP: 20 minutes
STAND: 30 minutes
CHILL: 1 hour
MAKES: 10 (generous 2-tablespoon) servings

1	cup finely shredded Gouda cheese (4 ounces)
¼	cup sour cream
¼	cup very finely chopped pecans Assorted small crackers and/or vegetable slices, for serving

1. In medium-size bowl, let cheese stand at room temperature for 30 minutes. Add sour cream and pecans. With electric mixer on medium speed, beat until ingredients are combined and mixture is creamy. Cover and refrigerate for up to 1 hour. If mixture is too firm, let stand for a few minutes to soften before piping.

2. To serve, spoon cheese mixture into a pastry bag fitted with ½-inch star tip. Pipe mixture onto assorted small crackers and/or vegetable slices.

Per serving: 104 cal., 10 g total fat (3 g sat.), 15 mg chol., 96 mg sodium, 2 g carbo., 1 g fiber, 4 g pro.

Chapter 2

Bring On Breakfast

Morning Glories

Whether you host a celebratory brunch or enjoy a slow Saturday morning, start your day deliciously with these hearty egg dishes, tempting baked goods and luscious fruit recipe.

Caramel-Pecan French Toast

Sour Cream Buns

It is fitting that Marie Beesley, who has farmed with her husband for almost 60 years in wheat-growing Kansas, would contribute a yeast bread recipe to her community cookbook, *Gove County Gleanings*. These treats are like cinnamon rolls, only better. The sour cream makes the rolls extra tender and rich. "It's nice to know family recipes are saved," Marie says.

PREP: 35 minutes
RISE: 45 minutes
BAKE: at 400° about 15 minutes
MAKES: 12 buns

1	package active dry yeast
¼	cup warm water (105° to 115°)
1	cup sour cream
3	tablespoons granulated sugar
2	tablespoons solid vegetable shortening
1	teaspoon salt
⅛	teaspoon baking soda
1	egg
3	to 3¼ cups all-purpose flour
2	tablespoons butter, softened
⅓	cup packed light-brown sugar
1	teaspoon ground cinnamon
¾	cup confectioners' sugar
2	to 4 teaspoons water

1. In large bowl, dissolve yeast in warm water. In saucepan, combine sour cream, granulated sugar, shortening and salt. Cook and stir over medium-low heat until mixture is warm (120° to 130°). Stir in baking soda. Stir sour cream mixture and egg into yeast. Stir in as much flour as possible. Turn dough out onto lightly floured surface; knead in enough of the remaining flour to make moderately soft dough (3 to 5 minutes total). Cover; let rest for 5 minutes.

2. Grease 12 cups of a standard muffin pan. On lightly floured surface, roll dough into 18×12-inch rectangle. Spread butter over dough. Combine brown sugar and cinnamon; sprinkle evenly over dough. Starting with a long side, roll dough into a spiral. Moisten and pinch seam. Cut into twelve 1½-inch slices. Place slices, cut sides down, in prepared muffin cups. Cover; let rise in a warm place until ¼ to ½ inch above tops of cups, about 45 minutes.

3. Heat oven to 400°. Bake buns about 15 minutes or until golden brown. Remove to wire racks and cool slightly. Combine confectioners' sugar and enough water to achieve thin consistency. Drizzle over rolls. Serve warm.

Per bun: 250 cal., 9 g total fat (4 g sat.), 32 mg chol., 246 mg sodium, 38 g carbo., 1 g fiber, 4 g pro.

Sour Cream Buns

Crunchy Toffee Mini Muffins

Like mothers everywhere, Wendy Vallelunga wants the best for her children. She contributed this simple recipe to a cookbook that supports the Foundation for Educational Excellence in Twain Harte, California. The fund provides grants to teachers for student field trips. For Wendy and the other mothers in Twain Harte, good food serves good causes.

PREP: 20 minutes
BAKE: at 400° about 12 minutes
MAKES: 36 mini muffins

1½	cups all-purpose flour
⅓	cup packed light-brown sugar
1	teaspoon baking powder
½	teaspoon baking soda
½	teaspoon salt
1	egg, beaten
½	cup milk
½	cup sour cream
3	tablespoons butter, melted
1	teaspoon vanilla extract
3	bars (1.4 ounces each) chocolate-covered English toffee, finely chopped

1. Heat oven to 400°. Grease 36 cups of miniature-size muffin pans or line with paper liners.

2. In medium-size bowl, combine flour, brown sugar, baking powder, baking soda and salt. Make a well in the center of flour mixture.

3. In another medium-size bowl, combine egg, milk, sour cream, melted butter and vanilla. Add all at once to the flour mixture. Stir just until moistened. Gently fold two-thirds of the finely chopped toffee bars into batter.

4. Spoon batter into prepared muffin cups, dividing batter evenly (cups will be full). Sprinkle remaining toffee bar pieces evenly over tops.

5. Bake at 400° about 12 minutes or until golden brown. Cool in muffin cups on a wire rack for 5 minutes. Loosen edges of muffins with a narrow metal spatula. Serve warm.

Per mini muffin: 62 cal., 3 g total fat (1 g sat.), 11 mg chol., 88 mg sodium, 8 g carbo., 0 g fiber, 1 g pro.

Crunchy Toffee Mini Muffins

Trifle Fruit Salad

Trifle Fruit Salad

The Alderson Gym in Twain Harte, California, bears the name of Adrienne Alderson, who served on the school board for 30 years, and also helped found the Foundation for Educational Excellence. She donated this recipe to a cookbook, the proceeds of which provide grants to teachers to support learning. That's no trifle.

PREP: 30 minutes
CHILL: 2 to 8 hours
MAKES: 10 to 12 serving

2	cups 1-inch chunks fresh pineapple or 1 can (20 ounces) pineapple chunks, drained
2	cups sliced fresh strawberries
2	cups fresh or frozen blueberries, thaw (if frozen)
2	cups seedless green grapes
1	box (about 3 ounces) instant banana cream pudding mix
1¼	cups milk
½	cup sour cream
1	can (8 ounces) crushed pineapple
	Sliced fresh strawberries and/or fresh blueberries, for garnish

1. In 2-quart trifle bowl or clear glass bowl, layer pineapple chunks, the 2 cups strawberries, the 2 cups blueberries and the grapes.

2. In medium-size bowl, whisk together dry pudding mix, milk and sour cream. Stir in crushed pineapple. Pour over the layered fruit. Cover and refrigerate for 2 to 8 hours.

3. To serve, garnish with additional strawberries and/or blueberries.

Per serving: 159 cal., 3 g total fat (2 g sat.), 7 mg chol., 172 mg sodium, 33 g carbo., 3 g fiber, 2 g pro.

Waffle Breakfast Casserole

Twelve-year-old Justin Michaels, of O'Fallon, Missouri, is proof that kids can win recipe contests. He won a trip to Disney World for his family and a freezer full of waffles when he collected the top prize for this recipe in the Kellogg's Eggo waffle contest. On the plane home from Florida, Justin received applause when a flight attendant announced his accomplishment.

PREP: 15 minutes
BAKE: at 350° for 50 to 60 minutes
CHILL: 4 to 24 hours
STAND: 10 minutes
MAKES: 8 servings

6	**frozen waffles, toasted and cubed**
1	**pound bulk pork sausage**
1	**cup shredded Cheddar cheese (4 ounces)**
6	**eggs, lightly beaten**
2	**cups milk**
1	**teaspoon dry mustard**
⅛	**teaspoon black pepper**
	Frozen waffles, toasted, for serving (optional)
	Maple syrup, for serving (optional)

1. In large skillet, cook sausage until brown. Drain off fat.

2. In ungreased 11×7×1½-inch baking dish, arrange half of the cubed waffles. Top with half of the sausage and about ⅓ cup of the cheese. Repeat layers of waffles and sausage.

3. In medium-size bowl, combine eggs, milk, mustard and pepper. Slowly pour egg mixture over layers in dish. Cover and refrigerate for 4 to 24 hours.

4. Heat oven to 350°. Bake, uncovered, at 350° for 50 to 60 minutes or until a knife inserted near center comes out clean. Remove from oven to wire rack. Sprinkle with remaining cheese. Let stand for 10 minutes before serving.

5. To serve, cut into rectangles. If desired, serve with toasted waffles and maple syrup.

Per serving: 413 cal., 28 g total fat (12 g sat.), 217 mg chol., 668 mg sodium, 15 g carbo., 1 g fiber, 19 g pro.

Waffle Breakfast Casserole

Creamy Caramel-Pecan Rolls

Frozen bread dough is a sweet shortcut for making these cinnamon-filled, caramel-topped rolls. Pictured on the front cover.

PREP: 25 minutes
RISE: 60 minutes
BAKE: at 375° for 20 to 25 minutes
STAND: 5 minutes
MAKES: 24 rolls

Topping:
- 1¼ cups confectioners' sugar
- ⅓ cup heavy cream
- 1 cup coarsely chopped pecans

Filling:
- ½ cup packed brown sugar
- 1 tablespoon ground cinnamon

Rolls:
- 2 16-ounce loaves frozen white bread dough or sweet roll dough, thawed
- 3 tablespoons butter or margarine, melted
- ¾ cup raisins (optional)

1. Generously grease two 9×1½-inch round baking pans. Line bottoms with a circle of parchment paper or nonstick foil; set pans aside.

2. Topping: In small bowl, combine confectioners' sugar and heavy cream. Divide mixture evenly between prepared baking pans gently spreading. Sprinkle pecans evenly over sugar mixture.

3. Filling: In another small bowl, combine brown sugar and cinnamon; set aside.

4. Rolls: On lightly floured surface, roll each loaf of dough into 12×8-inch rectangle. Brush with melted butter; sprinkle with brown sugar-cinnamon mixture. If desired, sprinkle with raisins. Starting with a long side, roll each dough rectangle into a spiral. Moisten and pinch seam. Cut each roll into 12 slices. Place slices, cut sides down, on topping in pans. Cover; let rise in a warm place until nearly double, about 60 minutes.

5. Preheat oven to 375°. Break any surface bubbles with a greased toothpick. Bake for 20 to 25 minutes or until rolls sound hollow when gently tapped (if necessary, cover rolls with foil the last 10 minutes of baking to prevent overbrowning). Cool in pans on wire rack for 5 minutes. Loosen edges and carefully invert rolls onto a serving platter. Spoon on any nut mixture that may remain in pan. Serve warm.

Per roll: 183 cal., 6 g total fat (2 g sat.), 8 mg chol., 13 mg sodium, 27 g carbo., 1 g fiber, 3 g pro.

Turkey Sausage Strata

The combination of green broccoli and red pimiento looks lovely and makes this a perfect choice for Christmas breakfast. The most beautiful thing of all? You can assemble the casserole the day before.

PREP: 25 minutes
BAKE: at 325° about 1 hour
CHILL: 2 to 24 hours
STAND: 10 minutes
MAKES: 12 servings

1	**pound bulk turkey sausage**
1	**medium-size onion, chopped**
12	**slices white bread**
1	**package (9 ounces) frozen cut broccoli, thawed and well drained**
1	**cup shredded mozzarella cheese (4 ounces)**
1	**jar (2 ounces) sliced pimiento, drained**
6	**eggs, beaten, or 1½ cups frozen or refrigerated egg product (thaw if frozen)**
3	**cups milk**
½	**teaspoon salt**
¼	**teaspoon dry mustard**
	Grated Parmesan cheese

1. Grease 13×9×2-inch baking dish. In large skillet, cook sausage and onion until meat is brown. Drain off fat.

2. In prepared baking dish, layer 6 slices white bread, half the sausage, half the broccoli, half the mozzarella and half the pimiento. Repeat layers.

3. In medium-size bowl, combine eggs, milk, salt and dry mustard. Slowly pour egg mixture evenly over layers in dish. With the back of large spoon, lightly press to moisten all bread. Cover and refrigerate for 2 to 24 hours.

4. Heat oven to 325°. Bake, uncovered, at 325° about 1 hour or until knife inserted near center comes out clean. Remove from oven to wire rack. Sprinkle with Parmesan cheese. Let stand for 10 minutes before serving. To serve, cut into squares.

Per serving: 238 cal., 11 g total fat (4 g sat.), 146 mg chol., 639 mg sodium, 19 g carbo., 1 g fiber, 17 g pro.

Zingy Cheese-and-Egg Casserole

This casserole puffs like a soufflé as it bakes, then sinks a little as it cools.

PREP: 35 minutes
CHILL: 8 to 24 hours
BAKE: at 325° for 45 to 50 minutes
STAND: 10 minutes
MAKES: 12 servings

1	loaf (16 ounces) French bread
1	package (8 ounces) cream cheese
8	strips bacon, crisp-cooked, drained and crumbled, or 1 cup diced cooked ham
1	can (4 ounces) chopped green chiles
1	cup shredded Cheddar cheese
1	cup shredded Monterey Jack cheese
10	eggs, beaten
2½	cups milk
1	teaspoon dry mustard

1. Grease 13×9×2-inch baking dish. Cut or tear bread into 1-inch pieces (about 15 cups). Place in prepared baking dish. Cut cream cheese into small cubes; layer cubes on top of bread. Sprinkle with bacon and chiles. Sprinkle with shredded cheeses.

2. In large bowl, with a rotary beater or wire whisk, beat eggs. Beat in milk and mustard. Slowly pour egg mixture over mixture in baking dish. With back of large metal spoon, lightly press bread to moisten all of it. Cover and refrigerate for 8 to 24 hours.

3. Heat oven to 325°. Bake, uncovered, at 325° for 45 to 50 minutes or until casserole is puffed and a knife inserted near center comes out clean. Remove from oven to wire rack; let stand for 10 minutes before serving. To serve, cut into squares.

Per serving: 356 cal., 21 g total fat (11 g sat.), 223 mg chol., 566 mg sodium, 24 g carbo., 1 g fiber, 18 g pro.

Vegetable Frittata

Packed full of colorful vegetables, this fresh-flavored, low-cal baked egg dish is perfect for brunch.

PREP: 25 minutes
BAKE: at 350° about 35 minutes
STAND: 10 minutes
MAKES: 8 servings

1½	pounds fresh asparagus, ends trimmed, cut into 1-inch pieces
1	medium-size sweet yellow pepper, cut into ¼-inch strips
1	small onion, chopped
1	small zucchini, halved lengthwise and sliced crosswise ¼ inch thick
10	eggs, lightly beaten
1	cup half-and-half
2	tablespoons chopped fresh flat-leaf parsley leaves
1¼	teaspoons salt
¼	to ½ teaspoon black pepper

1. Heat oven to 350°. Grease 11×7×1½-inch baking dish. In saucepan, bring about 1 inch water to a boil. Add asparagus, pepper strips and onion; bring just to a boil. Reduce heat; cover and boil about 1 minute or until crisp-tender. Drain well, reserving some asparagus tips for garnish, if desired. Spread asparagus-pepper mixture evenly in baking dish. Layer zucchini slices over asparagus mixture.

2. In medium-size bowl, combine eggs, half-and-half, parsley, salt and pepper. Pour egg mixture evenly over vegetables in baking dish. Bake, uncovered, at 350° about 35 minutes or until a knife inserted near center comes out clean. Remove to wire rack; let stand for 10 minutes before serving. If desired, garnish each serving with reserved asparagus tips.

Per serving: 160 cal., 10 g total fat (4 g sat), 277 mg chol., 465 mg sodium, 6 g carbo., 1 g fiber, 11 g pro.

Vegetable Frittata

Country Ham Quiche

With a simple tweak or two, this traditional quiche can go ethnic. Give it an Italian touch with fontina and provolone cheeses and a tablespoon of slivered fresh basil leaves—or make it Mexican with Monterey Jack instead of mozzarella, and top with salsa and sour cream.

PREP: 20 minutes
BAKE: at 350° for 45 to 50 minutes
STAND: 15 minutes
MAKES: 6 servings

1¼	cups all-purpose flour
¼	teaspoon salt
⅓	cup solid vegetable shortening
4	to 5 tablespoons cold water
4	eggs, lightly beaten
1	cup half-and-half
1	cup finely chopped country or smoked ham
½	cup shredded Cheddar cheese (2 ounces)
½	cup shredded mozzarella cheese (2 ounces)
½	teaspoon cracked black pepper
⅛	teaspoon cayenne pepper
	Fresh thyme sprigs, for garnish

1. Heat oven to 350°. In small bowl, combine flour and salt. With a pastry blender, cut in shortening until pieces are pea-size. Sprinkle 1 tablespoon cold water over part of flour mixture; gently toss with a fork. Push moistened dough to side of bowl. Repeat moistening dough, using 1 tablespoon cold water at a time, until all of dough is moistened. Form dough into ball. On lightly floured surface, use your hands to slightly flatten dough. Roll dough from center to edge into 12-inch circle. To transfer pastry, wrap it around the rolling pin. Unroll pastry into a 9-inch pie plate. Trim pastry to ½ inch beyond edge of pie plate. Turn under extra pastry. Crimp edge.

2. In medium-size bowl, with a wire whisk, whisk together eggs and half-and-half. Stir in ham, Cheddar cheese, mozzarella cheese, black pepper and cayenne pepper. Pour mixture into crust.

3. Bake at 350° for 45 to 50 minutes or until a knife inserted near center comes out clean. Remove from oven to wire rack; let stand for 15 minutes before serving. To serve, cut quiche into wedges. If desired, garnish with a thyme sprig.

Per serving: 393 cal., 26 g total fat (10 g sat.), 186 mg chol., 608 mg sodium, 21 g carbo., 1 g fiber, 18 g pro.

Easy Orange Rolls

These yummy rolls are filled and frosted with the same creamy orange combination of confectioners' sugar, orange juice, orange peel and butter.

PREP: 40 minutes
RISE: 30 minutes
BAKE: at 350° for 18 to 20 minutes
CHILL: 2 to 24 hours
MAKES: 18 standard or 12 jumbo rolls

1	package active dry yeast
¼	cup warm water (105°F to 115°F)
¼	cup granulated sugar
4	tablespoons (½ stick) butter or solid vegetable shortening
1¼	teaspoons salt
¾	cup boiling water
1	egg, lightly beaten
3	to 3½ cups all-purpose flour
1½	cups confectioners' sugar
3	tablespoons butter, melted
½	teaspoon finely shredded orange peel
1	to 2 tablespoons orange juice

1. In small bowl, dissolve yeast in the ¼ cup warm water. In large bowl, combine granulated sugar, the 4 tablespoons butter and the salt; add the ¾ cup boiling water, stirring to dissolve sugar and melt butter. Let stand until temperature is 105° to 115°. Stir in yeast mixture, egg and 1½ cups of the flour. With a wooden spoon, beat until a smooth dough forms. Stir in another 1½ cups flour. Gradually stir in enough of the remaining flour to make a dough that leaves the sides of bowl. (Dough will be soft.) Transfer to greased bowl, turning once to grease surface. Cover with plastic wrap and refrigerate for 2 to 24 hours.

2. In medium-size bowl, combine confectioners' sugar, melted butter, orange peel and enough of the orange juice to achieve spreading consistency. Cover.

3. Punch dough down; cover and let rest 10 minutes. Grease 18 cups of standard muffin pans. On lightly floured surface, roll dough into 12×8-inch rectangle. Spread half of the orange mixture to within ½ inch of edges; cover remaining orange mixture and set aside. Starting with a long side, roll dough into a spiral. Moisten the seam, and, using your fingers, pinch the seam to seal. Using sharp knife, cut into 18 slices. Place slices, cut sides down, in prepared muffin cups. Cover; let rise in a warm place until nearly doubled, about 30 minutes.

4. Heat oven to 350°. Bake, uncovered, at 350° for 18 to 20 minutes or until golden brown. Remove rolls to wire racks; cool slightly. Spread with remaining orange mixture. Serve warm.

Per roll: 162 cal., 5 g total fat (2 g sat.), 17 mg chol., 187 mg sodium, 26 g carbo., 1 g fiber, 3 g pro.

Caramel-Pecan French Toast

Pictured on page 29.

PREP: 20 minutes
BAKE: at 350° for 30 to 40 minutes
STAND: 10 minutes
CHILL: 8 to 24 hours
MAKES: 9 servings

1	cup packed light-brown sugar
½	cup (1 stick) butter
2	tablespoons light corn syrup
1	cup chopped pecans
36	to 40 half-inch slices baguette-style French bread
6	eggs, lightly beaten
1½	cups milk
1	teaspoon vanilla extract
1	tablespoon granulated sugar
1½	teaspoons ground cinnamon
¼	teaspoon ground nutmeg

1. In saucepan, combine brown sugar, butter and corn syrup. Over medium heat, cook, stirring, until butter is melted and brown sugar is dissolved. Pour into a 13×9×2-inch baking dish. Sprinkle with half of the pecans. Arrange half of the bread slices in a single layer in dish. Sprinkle with remaining pecans, and top with remaining bread slices.

2. In medium-size bowl, combine eggs, milk and vanilla extract. Slowly pour over bread. Press lightly with back of a large spoon to moisten bread.

3. In small bowl, combine granulated sugar, cinnamon and nutmeg; sprinkle evenly over bread. Cover and refrigerate for 8 to 24 hours.

4. Heat oven to 350°. Bake, uncovered, for 30 to 40 minutes or until light brown. Let stand for 10 minutes before serving. To serve, with a wide spatula, remove servings and invert onto plates.

Per serving: 499 cal., 25 g total fat (9 g sat.), 174 mg chol., 494 mg sodium, 59 g carbo., 3 g fiber, 11 g pro.

Topped Coconut Waffles

These chocolate-topped waffles make a decadent treat for breakfast—or a fabulous dessert after a "light" meal.

PREP: 15 minutes
BAKE: 3 minutes per waffle
MAKES: 8 waffles

1¾	cups all-purpose flour
2	tablespoons granulated sugar
1	tablespoon baking powder
	Pinch of salt
3	eggs, lightly beaten
1	can (14 ounces) unsweetened coconut milk
6	tablespoons (¾ stick) butter, melted
¾	cup sweetened flaked coconut
½	cup chocolate-flavor ice cream topping
½	cup chopped toasted almonds
	Sweetened whipped cream or confectioners' sugar, for serving (optional)

1. In medium-size bowl, combine flour, sugar, baking powder and salt. Make a well in center of flour mixture. In another medium-size bowl, mix eggs, coconut milk and butter. Stir in coconut. Add egg mixture all at once to flour mixture. Stir just until moistened. Batter should be slightly lumpy.

2. Lightly grease waffle baker; heat. Pour ½ cup batter onto prepared grids. Bake according to manufacturer's directions about 3 minutes or until golden brown. With a fork, lift waffle off grid. Repeat with remaining batter.

3. Drizzle waffles with topping and sprinkle with almonds. If desired, top with whipped cream or sprinkle with confectioners' sugar. Serve warm.

Per waffle: 453 cal., 28 g total fat (18 g sat.), 102 mg chol., 253 mg sodium, 43 g carbo., 3 g fiber, 9 g pro.

Topped Coconut Waffles

Coffee Coffee Cake

Can't get enough java? Drink your coffee and eat it too in this coffee-flavored breakfast treat.

PREP: 30 minutes
BAKE: at 350° about 30 minutes
MAKES: 9 servings

Cake:
⅓	cup granulated sugar
2	tablespoons instant coffee crystals
1½	teaspoons ground cinnamon
1½	cups all-purpose flour
½	cup granulated sugar
1	teaspoon baking powder
½	teaspoon baking soda
⅛	teaspoon salt
1	egg, lightly beaten
1	cup plain yogurt
3	tablespoons butter, melted
1	teaspoon vanilla extract
¼	cup finely chopped walnuts

Icing:
2	teaspoons instant coffee crystals
2	teaspoons milk
⅓	cup confectioners' sugar

1. Cake: Heat oven to 350°. Grease bottom and ½ inch up sides of 8×8×2-inch baking pan. In small bowl, combine the ⅓ cup granulated sugar, the 2 tablespoons coffee crystals and the cinnamon.

2. In large bowl, combine flour, the ½ cup granulated sugar, the baking powder, baking soda and salt. In medium-size bowl, combine egg, yogurt, melted butter and vanilla. Add egg mixture to flour mixture; stir until moistened. Spread half of the batter in prepared pan. Sprinkle with half of the sugar-coffee mixture. Repeat layers. Use a knife to swirl batter slightly. Sprinkle with nuts.

3. Bake at 350° about 30 minutes or until a wooden toothpick inserted in center comes out clean. Cool cake in pan on wire rack.

4. Icing: In small bowl, dissolve the 2 teaspoons coffee crystals in milk; stir in confectioners' sugar until smooth. Drizzle over coffee cake. Serve warm.

Per serving: 253 cal., 7 g total fat (3 g sat.), 35 mg chol., 198 mg sodium, 43 g carbo., 1 g fiber, 3 g pro.

Apricot-Almond Coffee Cake

PREP: 15 minutes
BAKE: at 350° for 55 to 60 minutes
STAND: 10 minutes
MAKES: 12 to 15 servings

Cake:

2	**cups all-purpose flour**
1	**teaspoon baking powder**
¼	**teaspoon salt**
1	**cup (2 sticks) butter, softened**
2	**cups granulated sugar**
2	**eggs**
1	**cup sour cream**
1	**teaspoon almond extract**
⅓	**cup apricot preserves**
⅓	**cup sliced almonds, toasted**

Icing:

1½	**cups confectioners' sugar**
4	**teaspoons milk**
¼	**teaspoon vanilla extract**

1. Cake: Heat oven to 350°. Grease and lightly flour a 10-inch fluted tube pan. Combine flour, baking powder and salt. Beat butter on medium speed for 30 seconds. Add granulated sugar gradually; beat until light and fluffy. Beat in eggs, one at a time, beating well after each. Beat in sour cream and almond extract. Beat in flour mixture until smooth.

2. Spoon half of the batter into prepared pan. Spoon apricot preserves over batter, being careful not to let preserves touch sides of pan. Sprinkle with almonds. Spoon remaining batter over almonds.

3. Bake at 350° for 55 to 60 minutes or until cake tests done. Let cake cool in pan on wire rack for 10 minutes. Remove cake from pan to wire rack.

4. Icing: Mix confectioners' sugar, milk and vanilla extract. Add more milk as needed to reach drizzling consistency. Drizzle over cake. Serve warm or cool.

Per serving: 492 cal., 22 g total fat (13 g sat. fat), 84 mg chol., 203 mg sodium, 70 g carbo., 1 g fiber, 5 g pro.

Carrot-Bran Muffins

These muffins are loaded with good stuff. The big-batch recipe makes enough batter for 30 standard-size muffins. Bake them up fresh a few at a time, or prepare them all at once and freeze for up to 3 months.

PREP: 20 minutes
BAKE: at 400° for 18 to 20 minutes
CHILL: up to 3 days
MAKES: 30 muffins

2½	**cups all-purpose flour**
2½	**cups whole bran cereal**
1½	**cups sugar**
2½	**teaspoons baking soda**
1	**teaspoon salt**
2	**cups buttermilk**
½	**cup vegetable oil**
2	**eggs, lightly beaten**
1½	**cups finely shredded carrots**
1½	**cups chopped walnuts**
1	**cup chopped dates**
1	**cup raisins**

1. In very large bowl, combine flour, bran cereal, sugar, baking soda and salt. In medium-size bowl, combine buttermilk, oil and eggs. Stir egg mixture into flour mixture just until combined. In medium-size bowl, combine carrots, walnuts, dates and raisins. Fold into batter just until combined. Cover and refrigerate for up to 3 days.

2. Grease 30 cups of standard muffin pans. Spoon batter into prepared cups. Fill cups two-thirds full.

3. Heat oven to 400°. Bake at 400° for 18 to 20 minutes or until golden brown. Cool in muffin cups for 5 minutes. Remove muffins to wire racks; serve warm.

Per muffin: 204 cal., 8 g total fat (1 g sat.), 15 mg chol., 218 mg sodium, 32 g carbo., 3 g fiber, 4 g pro.

Chapter 3

Lickety Split

Meals In Minutes

Dinner in 30 minutes or less? Why not? These first-rate family favorites will help you produce a hot, homemade meal any night of the week—and still have time to spare.

Salmon au Poivre

Pan-Seared Lamb Chops with Mint Salad

Pan-Seared Lamb Chops with Mint Salad

When Matthew Buchanan first bumped elbows with his mother in the kitchen, the 10-year-old was put in charge of the potatoes. "My family had to eat 100 varieties of au gratin," he says. Now a graduate of the Culinary Institute of America, Matthew still loves to come home to cook with Mom. This quick and fresh recipe shows he is as inventive as ever.

PREP: 15 minutes
COOK: 8 to 10 minutes
MAKES: 4 servings

- ¼ **cup chopped fresh mint leaves**
- ¼ **cup chopped fresh flat-leaf parsley leaves**
- ¼ **cup crumbled feta cheese (1 ounce)**
- ¼ **cup chopped pecans, toasted**
- 8 **lamb rib chops or loin chops, cut 1 inch thick (about 2 pounds total)**
- 2 **teaspoons olive oil**
- ¼ **teaspoon salt**
- ⅛ **teaspoon black pepper**
  Olive oil (optional)
  Lemon juice (optional)
  Mixed salad greens, for serving (optional)

1. In small bowl, combine mint, parsley, feta cheese and pecans.

2. Trim fat from chops. Rub chops with the 2 teaspoons olive oil, salt and pepper. Heat heavy large skillet over medium-high heat until very hot. Add chops. For medium-rare doneness, cook chops, turning once halfway through cooking, for 8 to 10 minutes or until chops are well browned and an instant-read meat thermometer inserted in the thickest portion registers 145°.

3. To serve, sprinkle chops with mint mixture. If desired, drizzle olive oil and/or lemon juice over mint mixture and serve with salad greens.

Per serving: 252 cal., 17 g total fat (5 g sat.), 72 mg chol., 311 mg sodium, 2 g carbo., 1 g fiber, 22 g pro.

Mediterranean Mostaccioli

It can be a challenge to avoid mealtime monotony when you're chief cook and bottle washer at home—and a working parent too. Like many working parents, LaRee Hawks of Des Moines comes home to hungry kids and a need for creative dinner ideas. Her Mediterranean Mostaccioli is a pasta dish with a flavor twist to keep things interesting.

PREP: 10 minutes
COOK: about 15 minutes
MAKES: 4 to 6 servings

¼	pound mostaccioli or gemelli pasta
2	cups sliced zucchini
½	pound ground beef
½	medium eggplant, peeled and cubed (about 2½ cups)
1	can (14½ ounces) diced tomatoes with basil, oregano and garlic
2	tablespoons tomato paste
½	cup shredded carrot
¼	cup chopped fresh basil leaves
2	tablespoons raisins (optional)
¼	teaspoon ground cinnamon
1	tablespoon balsamic vinegar (optional)
½	cup shredded mozzarella cheese (2 ounces)

1. Cook pasta following package directions, adding zucchini during the last 2 minutes of cooking. Drain; keep warm.

2. In large skillet, cook beef and eggplant over medium heat until meat is brown. Drain off fat. Stir in undrained tomatoes, tomato paste, carrot, basil, raisins (if desired) and cinnamon. Bring to a boil. Reduce heat; simmer, uncovered, about 2 minutes or until mixture reaches desired consistency, stirring occasionally. Remove from heat. If desired, stir in vinegar.

3. Transfer pasta mixture to serving dish. Spoon sauce over pasta mixture. Sprinkle with cheese.

Per serving: 334 cal., 11 g total fat (5 g sat. fat), 47 mg chol., 672 mg sodium, 38 g carbo., 4 g fiber, 21 g pro.

Mediterranean Mostaccioli

Killer Omelets

You can leave out the jalapeño, if you like, and this omelet will still be "killer."

PREP: 15 minutes
COOK: about 5 minutes per omelet
MAKES: 4 servings

1	**small green pepper and/or sweet red pepper, seeded and chopped (⅔ cup)**
1	**fresh jalapeño chile, seeded and finely chopped***
	Bacon drippings or olive oil
1	**medium-size tomato, seeded and chopped**
6	**eggs**
¼	**cup heavy cream**
¼	**cup shredded Cheddar cheese (1 ounce)**
¼	**cup shredded Swiss cheese (1 ounce)**

1. In 10-inch nonstick skillet with flared sides, cook green and/or red pepper and chile pepper in 1 tablespoon bacon drippings over medium heat for 2 to 3 minutes or until tender. Stir in tomato. Remove vegetable mixture from skillet.

2. In medium-size bowl, whisk together eggs and cream. In same skillet, heat 1 teaspoon bacon drippings over medium heat. Add half of the egg mixture to skillet. Cook, pushing cooked eggs into center of skillet and tilting skillet to coat with uncooked mixture.

3. When eggs are set but still shiny, spoon half of the vegetable mixture across center of omelet. Sprinkle filling with half of the Cheddar cheese and half of the Swiss cheese. Fold sides over. Heat for 1 to 2 minutes more to melt cheeses. Transfer omelet to a serving plate; keep warm. Repeat with another 1 teaspoon bacon drippings and remaining egg mixture, vegetable mixture and cheeses.

***Note:** Jalapeños and other hot chiles contain oils that can burn your skin and eyes. Avoid direct contact with them as much as possible. When working with hot chiles, wear plastic or rubber gloves. If your bare hands do touch the chiles, wash your hands well with soap and warm water.

Per serving: 280 cal., 23 g total fat (11 g sat.), 359 mg chol., 166 mg sodium, 5 g carbo., 0 g fiber, 14 g pro.

Killer Omelets

Apricot-Dijon Pork Salad

Apricot-Dijon Pork Salad

One delicious apricot-mustard dressing does double duty in this recipe. It functions as a basting sauce for the grilled pork and gets tossed with the salad greens too.

PREP: 12 minutes
GRILL: 16 to 18 minutes
MAKES: 4 servings

1	cup apricot preserves
¼	cup white-wine vinegar
2	tablespoons Dijon mustard
½	teaspoon ground ginger
1	pound pork tenderloin
10	cups spring greens or mesclun mix
1	can (15¼ ounces) apricot halves, drained and sliced
½	cup dried tart cherries
8	scallions, trimmed and cut into ½-inch pieces
¼	cup pecan pieces, toasted

1. Heat gas grill to medium-high or prepare charcoal grill with medium-hot coals. Chop any large pieces of preserves. In small bowl, combine preserves, vinegar, mustard and ginger. Reserve ⅓ cup for brushing on pork; set aside remainder for dressing.

2. Cut tenderloin in half lengthwise almost to opposite side; open and lay flat. Place pork on grill; grill for 4 minutes. Turn pork over and grill for 4 minutes more. Brush top of pork with some of the ⅓ cup preserves mixture; grill for 4 minutes more. Turn pork over again and brush top with remaining preserves mixture. Grill about 4 to 6 minutes more or until an instant-read meat thermometer inserted in the thickest area of pork registers 155°.

3. Meanwhile, in bowl, combine greens, apricots, cherries, scallions and pecans. Divide among four plates. Slice pork ½ inch thick. Arrange pork on top of greens mixture; drizzle with remaining apricot mixture for dressing.

Per serving: 539 cal., 8 g total fat (2 g sat.), 73 mg chol., 272 mg sodium, 88 g carbo., 6 g fiber, 28 g pro.

Quick Skillet Lasagna

Love lasagna but don't have time to layer and bake it? The most time-consuming step of this clever stovetop lasagna is boiling the noodles.

PREP: 15 minutes
COOK: 5 to 7 minutes
STAND: 1 minute
MAKES: 6 servings

6	ounces ripple-edged mafalda (lasagna) noodles (3 cups)
¾	pound lean ground beef or bulk pork sausage
1	jar (26 to 28 ounces) tomato pasta sauce
1½	cups shredded mozzarella cheese (6 ounces)
¼	cup grated Parmesan cheese (1 ounce)

1. Cook pasta following package directions. Drain well.

2. In large nonstick skillet, cook meat until brown. Drain off fat; remove meat from pan. Wipe skillet clean with paper towels.

3. Place half of pasta in skillet. Cover with half of sauce. Spoon cooked meat over sauce. Sprinkle with 1 cup of the mozzarella cheese. Top with remaining pasta and sauce. Sprinkle remaining mozzarella and Parmesan cheese over top.

4. Cover and cook over medium heat for 5 to 7 minutes or until lasagna is heated through and cheese has melted. Remove skillet from heat; let stand, covered, for 1 minute.

Per serving: 375 cal., 17 g total fat (6 g sat.), 50 mg chol., 1,046 mg sodium, 30 g carbo., 2 g fiber, 25 g pro.

Italian Beef-Potato Pie

If you don't have a set of individual casserole dishes, layer the meat, potatoes and cheese in a 2-quart broilerproof casserole dish.

PREP: 10 minutes
COOK: about 10 minutes
BROIL: 2 to 3 minutes
MAKES: 6 servings

1	tablespoon vegetable oil
2	small zucchini or yellow summer squash, sliced crosswise
1	medium-size onion, chopped (½ cup)
1	package (17 ounces) refrigerated cooked beef tips with gravy
1	can (14½ ounces) diced tomatoes with basil, oregano and garlic, undrained
½	can (6 ounces) tomato paste (⅓ cup)
¼	teaspoon black pepper
2	cups refrigerated mashed potatoes
½	cup shredded pizza-blend cheese (2 ounces)
	Paprika (optional)

1. Heat broiler. In large skillet, heat oil over medium heat. Add zucchini and onion; cook until onion is tender. Stir in beef with gravy, tomatoes, tomato paste and pepper. Heat through. Divide meat mixture among six 10-ounce broilerproof casseroles.

2. Heat potatoes according to package directions. Spoon mashed potatoes into mounds on top of beef mixture. Sprinkle with cheese and, if desired, paprika.

3. Place casseroles on 15×10×1-inch baking pan. Broil 4 to 5 inches from heat for 2 to 3 minutes or until cheese is melted and brown.

Per serving: 249 cal., 9 g total fat (3 g sat.), 38 mg chol., 971 mg sodium, 24 g carbo., 2 g fiber, 18 g pro.

Chili Macaroni

Sicilian Meat Loaves

Kids love anything made with wagon wheel macaroni—it's just plain fun. This simple chili trades the traditional kidney beans for green beans to make a one-dish meal.

PREP: 15 minutes
COOK: 15 minutes
MAKES: 4 servings

¾	pound lean ground beef or uncooked ground turkey
1	medium-size onion, chopped (½ cup)
1	can (14½ ounces) diced tomatoes and green chiles, undrained
1¼	cups tomato juice
2	teaspoons chili powder
½	teaspoon garlic salt
1	cup wagon wheel macaroni or elbow macaroni
1	cup frozen cut green beans
1	cup shredded Cheddar cheese (4 ounces) (optional)
	Tortilla chips, for serving (optional)

1. In very large skillet, cook ground beef and onion over medium heat until meat is brown. Drain off fat. Stir undrained tomatoes, tomato juice, chili powder and garlic salt into meat mixture. Bring to a boil. Stir in macaroni and green beans. Return to a boil. Reduce heat; simmer, covered, about 15 minutes or until pasta and beans are tender.

2. If desired, sprinkle Cheddar cheese over mixture in skillet and serve with tortilla chips.

Per serving: 443 cal., 20 g total fat (9 g sat.), 83 mg chol., 881 mg sodium, 37 g carbo., 5 g fiber, 29 g pro.

These yummy miniature meat loaves cook in a fraction of the time that one big loaf does—and there's a surprise inside too.

PREP: 10 minutes
BAKE: at 400° about 20 minutes
MAKES: 4 servings

1	egg, beaten
1	jar (14 ounces) garlic and onion tomato pasta sauce (1¾ cups)
¼	cup packaged seasoned dry bread crumbs
¼	teaspoon salt
¼	teaspoon black pepper
¾	pound ground beef
2	ounces mozzarella cheese
4	thin slices prosciutto or cooked ham (about 2 ounces)
1	package (9 ounces) refrigerated plain or spinach fettuccine

1. Heat oven to 400°. In medium-size bowl, combine egg, ¼ cup of the pasta sauce, dry bread crumbs, salt and pepper. Add ground beef; mix. Cut mozzarella cheese into four logs, each about 2¼×¾×½ inches. Wrap a slice of prosciutto around each cheese log. Shape one-fourth of the ground beef mixture around each cheese log to form a loaf. Flatten each meat loaf to 1½ inches thick; arrange in a shallow baking pan.

2. Bake loaves at 400° about 20 minutes or until an instant-read meat thermometer registers 160° when inserted in the center of each loaf.

3. Cook pasta following package directions. Drain well. In small saucepan heat remaining 1½ cups pasta sauce over medium heat until bubbly. In large shallow serving bowl, arrange meat loaves over hot cooked pasta. Spoon sauce over top.

Per serving: 631 cal., 31 g total fat (12 g sat.), 173 mg chol., 1,132 mg sodium, 55 g carbo., 3 g fiber, 31 g pro.

Chili Macaroni

Quick Honey-Garlic Pot Roast

You can have comforting, Sunday-style pot roast any day of the week. Just start with precooked meat, add fresh vegetables, and dinner's on in 30 minutes.

PREP: 10 minutes
COOK: 20 to 25 minutes
MAKES: 4 servings

1	package (17 ounces) refrigerated cooked beef roast au jus or beef pot roast with juices
2	tablespoons honey
1	tablespoon Worcestershire sauce
1	to 1½ teaspoons bottled roasted chopped garlic
¼	teaspoon black pepper
2	cups packaged peeled baby carrots
¾	pound small red potatoes, quartered
1	medium-size red onion, cut into thin wedges
	Chopped fresh parsley leaves, for garnish (optional)

1. Remove meat from package, reserving juices. In medium-size bowl, combine reserved juices, honey, Worcestershire sauce, roasted garlic and pepper. In large nonstick skillet, place beef; arrange carrots, potatoes and onion wedges around beef. Pour honey mixture over beef and vegetables.

2. Bring mixture to a boil. Reduce heat; cook, covered, for 20 to 25 minutes or until vegetables are tender and meat is heated through.

3. To serve, transfer beef and vegetables to a serving platter. Spoon sauce over beef and vegetables. If desired, sprinkle with parsley.

Per serving: 305 cal., 9 g total fat (4 g sat.), 64 mg chol., 502 mg sodium, 35 g carbo., 4 g fiber, 26 g pro.

Peanut-Chicken Bowl

PREP: 15 minutes
COOK: about 10 minutes
MAKES: 4 servings

2 packages (3 ounces each) Oriental-flavored ramen noodles
3 cups cut assorted vegetables
1¼ cups water
¼ cup peanut butter
¼ cup soy sauce
2 tablespoons packed light-brown sugar
1 tablespoon cornstarch
½ teaspoon red pepper flakes
2 cups chopped cooked chicken
1 can (8 ounces) sliced water chestnuts, drained
1 can (8 ounces) bamboo shoots, drained
¼ cup chopped peanuts
¼ cup trimmed and sliced scallions

1. In large saucepan, bring 2 quarts water to a boil. Break up noodles slightly and add to water along with cut vegetables. Set aside 1 seasoning packet from noodles to use in recipe and save remaining packet for another use. Return mixture to a boil. Reduce heat; boil gently, uncovered, for 3 minutes. Drain mixture and return to saucepan.

2. In medium-size saucepan, whisk together the 1¼ cups water, peanut butter, soy sauce, brown sugar, cornstarch, pepper flakes and reserved seasoning packet until smooth. Cook and stir over medium heat until thick and bubbly. Cook and stir for 2 minutes more. Add chicken, water chestnuts and bamboo shoots to sauce; heat through. Add to noodle mixture in saucepan. Toss to combine. Serve immediately in bowls. Sprinkle each serving with peanuts and scallions.

Per serving: 646 cal., 30 g total fat (4 g sat.), 82 mg chol., 1,511 mg sodium, 64 g carbo., 6 g fiber, 38 g pro.

Creamy Ranch Chicken

Even if you don't normally drink whole milk, be sure to use it in this dish—it's what makes the sauce so creamy and delicious.

PREP: 20 minutes
COOK: about 8 minutes
MAKES: 4 servings

6 strips bacon
1 pound boneless, skinless chicken breasts, cut into bite-size pieces
2 tablespoons all-purpose flour
2 tablespoons dry ranch salad dressing mix
1¼ cups whole milk
3 cups medium-size egg noodles
1 tablespoon finely shredded Parmesan cheese

1. Cut bacon into narrow strips. In large skillet, cook bacon over medium heat until crisp. Drain bacon, reserving 2 tablespoons drippings in skillet. Discard remaining drippings.

2. Cook chicken, turning to brown evenly, in reserved drippings until no longer pink. Sprinkle flour and salad dressing mix over chicken in skillet; stir well. Stir in milk. Cook and stir until thickened and bubbly. Cook and stir 1 minute more. Stir in the bacon.

3. Cook noodles following package directions. Drain well. Serve chicken mixture with noodles and sprinkle with Parmesan cheese.

Per serving: 488 cal., 18 g total fat (7 g sat.), 137 mg chol., 574 mg sodium, 27 g carbo., 1 g fiber, 45 g pro.

Chicken and Bow Ties

This recipe calls for a splash of dry white wine. You'll have a lot left over, so select one you'd enjoy sipping with dinner. Chardonnay, Pinot Grigio or Sauvignon Blanc are all good choices.

PREP: 13 minutes
COOK: about 17 minutes
MAKES: 4 servings

½   pound farfalle (bow tie) pasta
2   tablespoons olive oil
2   cloves garlic, finely chopped
1   pound boneless, skinless chicken breasts, cut into thin bite-size strips
1   teaspoon dried basil
⅛   teaspoon red pepper flakes
¾   cup chicken broth
½   cup sun-dried tomatoes in oil, drained and cut into thin strips
¼   cup dry white wine
½   cup heavy cream
¼   cup grated Parmesan cheese
    Grated Parmesan cheese, for serving (optional)

1. Cook pasta following package directions. Drain well.

2. In large skillet, heat oil over medium-high heat. Add garlic and cook for 30 seconds. Add chicken, basil and pepper flakes. Cook and stir about 4 minutes or until chicken is brown. Add chicken broth, dried tomatoes and white wine. Bring to a boil. Reduce heat; cook, uncovered, about 10 minutes or until chicken is tender and no longer pink. Stir in cream and the ¼ cup Parmesan cheese; cook for 2 minutes more. Stir pasta into chicken mixture. Heat through. If desired, pass additional Parmesan cheese.

Per serving: 574 cal., 24 g total fat (10 g sat.), 112 mg chol., 414 mg sodium, 48 g carbo., 2 g fiber, 38 g pro.

Quick Fried Chicken with Strawberries

PREP: 20 minutes
COOK: 6 to 8 minutes
MAKES: 6 servings

¾   cup all-purpose flour
4   tablespoons chopped fresh basil leaves
1   tablespoon finely shredded lemon peel
2   eggs, beaten
1   pound boneless, skinless chicken breast strips
2   tablespoons vegetable oil
4   cups mixed spring salad greens
1   head radicchio, torn into bite-size pieces
2   cups sliced fresh strawberries
½   cup bottled balsamic vinaigrette
6   butterhead (Bibb or Boston) lettuce leaves

1. In shallow dish, combine flour, 2 tablespoons of the basil and the lemon peel. In another shallow dish, place eggs. Dip chicken into flour mixture, into eggs, and then again into flour mixture to coat.

2. In heavy very large skillet, heat oil over medium-high heat. Add chicken breast strips to skillet. Cook, turning once, for 6 to 8 minutes or until chicken is no longer pink. (If necessary to prevent overbrowning, reduce heat to medium. Add more oil as needed during cooking.) Cool slightly.

3. Meanwhile, in large bowl, toss together greens, radicchio, strawberries and remaining 2 tablespoons chopped basil. Drizzle vinaigrette over greens mixture; toss gently to coat.

4. To serve, line each of six bowls with lettuce leaves. Add greens mixture. Top with chicken.

Per serving: 261 cal., 13 g total fat (2 g sat.), 79 mg chol., 295 mg sodium, 16 g carbo., 2 g fiber, 21 g pro.

Mock Chicken Pot Pie

Something about chicken pot pie cures any ill and lifts any mood. This version of the country-style classic is ready in just about 25 minutes so you can feel good fast.

PREP: 10 minutes
BAKE: at 450° for 6 to 8 minutes
COOK: about 10 minutes
MAKES: 4 servings

Pastry Strips:
- ½ package (15 ounces) rolled refrigerated unbaked piecrusts, at room temperature (1 crust)

Filling:
- 1 can (10¾ ounces) condensed cream of onion soup
- 1⅓ cups reduced-fat milk
- 3 ounces reduced-fat cream cheese, cut up
- ½ teaspoon dried sage
- ¼ teaspoon black pepper
- 1½ cups chopped cooked chicken
- 1 package (10 ounces) frozen mixed vegetables
- ½ cup instant rice

1. Pastry Strips: Heat oven to 450°. Unroll piecrust. With pizza cutter or sharp knife, cut piecrust into strips about ½ to 1 inch wide. Place piecrust strips on baking sheet. Bake at 450° for 6 to 8 minutes or until golden.

2. Filling: In large saucepan, combine soup, milk, cream cheese, sage and pepper. Cook and stir over medium-high heat until cheese melts. Stir in chicken, vegetables and rice. Bring to a boil. Reduce heat; simmer, covered, about 10 minutes or until vegetables and rice are tender.

3. To serve, transfer filling to serving dish. Top with pastry strips.

Per serving: 587 cal., 27 g total fat (12 g sat.), 86 mg chol., 999 mg sodium, 58 g carbo., 2 g fiber, 25 g pro.

Skillet Tuna and Biscuits

Salmon au Poivre

Au poivre is French for "with the pepper." You can buy cracked pepper, or you can make your own with a pepper grinder on the coarse setting. Pictured on page 49.

PREP: 15 minutes
COOK: about 6 minutes
MAKES: 4 servings

4	skinless salmon fillets (about 6 ounces each)
¼	teaspoon salt
2	to 3 teaspoons cracked black pepper
2	tablespoons olive oil
½	cup chicken broth
1	package (5 to 6 ounces) torn mixed salad greens
1	cup halved fresh strawberries
¼	cup bottled balsamic vinaigrette
2	tablespoons honey

1. Sprinkle salmon fillets with salt. Lightly coat each side of salmon with cracked black pepper. In large skillet, heat oil over medium-high heat. Add salmon fillets to hot oil and cook for 1 minute. Turn salmon over and carefully add chicken broth. Bring to a boil. Reduce heat; cook, covered, about 5 minutes or until salmon flakes when tested with a fork.

2. Divide salad greens and strawberries among four dinner plates. Drizzle greens with vinaigrette. With a slotted spoon, remove salmon from cooking liquid and place on greens; drizzle honey over salmon.

Per serving: 467 cal., 30 g total fat (5 g sat.), 100 mg chol., 546 mg sodium, 15 g carbo., 1 g fiber, 35 g pro.

Skillet Tuna and Biscuits

This family-friendly dish is quick to fix and easy to clean up: It's cooked, baked and served in the same pan.

PREP: 15 minutes
BAKE: at 400° for 12 to 15 minutes
MAKES: 4 servings

1¼	cups reduced-fat Alfredo pasta sauce
1	package (10 ounces) frozen peas and carrots
1	can (4 ounces) sliced mushrooms, drained
1	teaspoon lemon juice
¼	teaspoon dried dill
1	can (12 ounces) tuna, drained and flaked
1	cup all-purpose baking mix (such as Bisquick)
⅓	cup fat-free milk
¼	cup shredded Cheddar cheese (1 ounce)

1. Heat oven to 400°. In large ovenproof skillet, combine pasta sauce, peas and carrots, mushrooms, lemon juice and dill. Cook and stir over medium heat until bubbly and heated through. Stir in tuna. Cover to keep warm.

2. In medium-size bowl, combine baking mix, milk and half of the cheese. Drop mixture into 4 mounds on top of tuna mixture. Sprinkle with the remaining cheese.

3. Bake at 400° for 12 to 15 minutes or until biscuits are golden. To serve, spoon some tuna mixture and a biscuit into each of four bowls.

Per serving: 434 cal., 22 g total fat (10 g sat. fat), 85 mg chol., 1,032 mg sodium, 32 g carbo., 3 g fiber, 29 g pro.

Chapter 4

Cook It Slowly

Slow Cooker Meals

Toss a few fresh ingredients in the slow cooker before you leave home for the day. When you return you will find a heartwarming, flavorful meal that is ready to eat when you are.

Easy Cheesy Potatoes

Family-Style Chili and Dumplings

Maryellyn Krantz of Des Moines makes good use of her slow cooker. She uses it to cook beef and pork for sandwiches, Mexican dishes and Tex-Mex favorites like this chili topped with cornmeal dumplings. As a tasty addition, Maryellyn tops the hearty bowls with shredded cheese and strips of scallion. Garnished or not, this recipe is easy and unexcelled.

PREP: 25 minutes
COOK: 8 to 10 hours on low-heat setting or
4 to 5 hours on high-heat setting, plus
20 to 25 minutes on high-heat setting
MAKES: 6 to 8 servings

Chili:
- 1 pound boneless beef round steak, trimmed and cut into ½-inch cubes
- 1 large onion, chopped
- 1 green pepper, seeded and chopped
- 1 can (15 ounces) chili beans with chili gravy
- 1 can (15 ounces) kidney or pinto beans, drained and rinsed
- 1 can (14½ ounces) Mexican-style stewed tomatoes, cut up
- 1 cup beef broth
- ¼ to ½ teaspoon red pepper flakes
- 1 teaspoon ground cumin
- ¾ teaspoon garlic salt
- ½ teaspoon dried oregano

Dumplings:
- 1 package (8 ounces) corn muffin mix
- ½ cup shredded Cheddar cheese
- 2 scallions, trimmed and sliced
- 1 egg, lightly beaten
- ¼ cup sour cream

1. Chili: In 3½- or 4-quart slow cooker, combine beef, onion, green pepper, beans, tomatoes, beef broth, pepper flakes, cumin, garlic salt and oregano. Cover slow cooker; cook on low-heat setting for 8 to 10 hours or on high-heat setting for 4 to 5 hours.

2. Dumplings: Combine muffin mix, cheese and scallions. Combine egg and sour cream. Stir egg mixture into cheese mixture. If using low-heat setting, turn to high-heat setting. If you have an oval slow cooker, drop all dumpling batter onto the bubbling mixture in slow cooker. (If you have a round cooker, heat oven to 400°. Drop half of the dumpling batter onto the bubbling mixture. Spoon remaining batter into two or three greased cups of a standard muffin pan. Bake at 400° for 15 to 18 minutes or until a toothpick inserted in the center comes out clean.) Cover slow cooker; cook for 20 to 25 minutes more or until a wooden toothpick inserted into dumplings comes out clean.

Per serving: 529 cal., 17 g total fat (6 g sat.), 101 mg chol., 1,256 mg sodium, 61 g carbo., 9 g fiber, 35 g pro.

Family-Style Chili and Dumplings

Party-Time Brisket

Some people love to sing for their supper. After Sue and Bruce Anderson and their musically inclined friends have sung the last note at their Christmas caroling stroll around their storybook town of Decorah, Iowa, they gather at the Andersons' house for a potluck feast. Sue's specialty is this yummy brisket that cooks while she sings her heart out.

PREP: 15 minutes
MARINATE: overnight
COOK: 10 to 12 hours on low-heat setting or
5 to 6 hours on high-heat setting
MAKES: 10 servings

1	fresh beef brisket (3 to 3½ pounds)
2	tablespoons liquid smoke
2	teaspoons celery seeds
2	teaspoons black pepper
2	teaspoons Worcestershire sauce
1	teaspoon garlic salt
1	teaspoon onion salt
½	cup water
10	buns or French-style rolls, split and toasted
1	cup bottled barbecue sauce

1. Trim fat from beef. In 13×9×2-inch baking dish, place beef.

2. In small bowl, combine liquid smoke, celery seeds, pepper, Worcestershire sauce, garlic salt and onion salt. Rub seasoning mixture on beef, coating all sides evenly. Cover and marinate beef in the refrigerator overnight.

3. In 4½- or 5-quart slow cooker, place beef. Pour the ½ cup water around brisket. Cover slow cooker; cook on low-heat setting for 10 to 12 hours or on high-heat setting for 5 to 6 hours.

4. Transfer beef to cutting board. Thinly slice beef across the grain. Arrange beef slices on roll bottoms. Drizzle with barbecue sauce. Add roll tops.

Per serving: 335 cal., 7 g total fat (2 sat.), 56 mg chol., 857 mg sodium, 31 g carbo., 1 g fiber, 34 g pro.

Party-Time Brisket

Shredded Pork Tacos

Shredded Pork Tacos

Ellen Boeke of Des Moines says her two sons are like Jack Sprat and his wife. One loves to sample new foods while the other would be content with hot dogs every night of the week. Ellen keeps everyone happy with recipes like this one that are easily customized. The adventuresome eaters use every topping while the less daring keep it simple.

PREP: 30 minutes
COOK: 8 to 10 hours on low-heat setting or
4 to 5 hours on high-heat setting
MAKES: 4 servings

1	**boneless pork shoulder roast (2½ to 3 pounds)**
1	**cup chicken broth**
½	**cup enchilada sauce or bottled salsa**
4	**(8-inch) flour tortillas or taco shells**
	Assorted toppers, such as shredded lettuce, finely shredded Mexican-blend cheese, chopped tomato, sliced pitted ripe olives and/or chopped avocado
	Sour cream, for serving (optional)

1. Trim fat from pork. If necessary, cut pork to fit in 3½- or 4-quart slow cooker. Place pork in cooker. Add broth.

2. Cover slow cooker; cook on low-heat setting for 8 to 10 hours or on high-heat setting for 4 to 5 hours. Remove pork from cooker; discard broth. Using forks, shred pork, discarding any fat. Reserve 2 cups of the pork. (Place remaining pork in an airtight container for another use; refrigerate up to 3 days or freeze up to 3 months.)

3. In medium-size saucepan, combine reserved 2 cups pork and enchilada sauce. Cover and cook over medium-low heat about 10 minutes or until heated through, stirring occasionally. Warm flour tortillas following package directions.

4. To assemble tacos, place pork mixture in center of warm tortillas or in taco shells. Top as desired with lettuce, cheese, tomato, olives and/or avocado. If desired, serve with sour cream.

Per serving: 616 cal., 31 g total fat (10 g sat.), 202 mg chol., 846 mg sodium, 20 g carbo., 3 g fiber, 61 g pro.

Savory Vegetable Stew

Englishwoman Ann Ackerman of Fort Scott, Kansas, says, "Gardening is something the English do." She uses the bounty from the garden she keeps with her husband, Milton, to make many inventive, fresh and flavorful recipes. The Ackermans have lived in many American cities and in New Zealand. They garden no matter where they reside.

PREP: 30 minutes
COOK: 10 to 12 hours on low-heat setting or
5 to 6 hours on high-heat setting, plus
15 minutes on high-heat setting
MAKES: 6 servings

1	large russet potato, peeled and cut into 1-inch cubes
1	medium-size sweet potato, peeled and cut into 1-inch cubes
1	large carrot, peeled and sliced
1	cup peeled rutabaga cut into ½-inch cubes
1	rib celery, coarsely chopped
5	boiling onions, peeled
1	can (15 ounces) chickpeas, drained and rinsed
2	ounces small button mushrooms, halved (½ cup)
1	teaspoon Cajun seasoning
1	can (14½ ounces) Mexican-style stewed tomatoes, cut up
1	can (14 ounces) vegetable broth

1	medium-size sweet red pepper, seeded and coarsely chopped
1	medium-size green pepper, seeded and coarsely chopped
1	cup frozen whole green beans
½	cup frozen peas

1. In 3½- or 4-quart slow cooker, combine potatoes, carrot, rutabaga, celery, onions, chickpeas, mushrooms and Cajun seasoning. Stir in tomatoes and vegetable broth.

2. Cover slow cooker; cook on low-heat setting for 10 to 12 hours or on high-heat setting for 5 to 6 hours.

3. If using low-heat setting, turn to high-heat setting. Add red and green pepper, green beans and frozen peas. Cover and cook for 15 minutes. To serve, ladle stew into bowls.

Per serving: 223 cal., 1 g total fat, (0 sat.), 0 mg chol., 799 mg sodium, 47 g carbo., 8 g fiber, 8 g pro.

Savory Vegetable Stew

Country Swiss Steak

You may have the time to whip up homemade mashed potatoes while this dish finishes slow cooking, but if you don't, pick up some frozen mashed potatoes at the supermarket. All you have to do is heat them in the microwave and serve 'em.

PREP: 20 minutes
COOK: 10 to 12 hours on low-heat setting or
5 to 6 hours on high-heat setting
MAKES: 4 servings

1	**pound boneless beef round steak, cut ¾ to 1 inch thick**
1	**tablespoon vegetable oil**
1	**small onion, sliced and separated into rings**
2	**tablespoons quick-cooking tapioca**
1	**teaspoon dried thyme**
¼	**teaspoon salt**
¼	**teaspoon black pepper**
1	**can (14½ ounces) chunky tomatoes with garlic and spices**
4	**cups hot mashed potatoes**
	Fresh thyme sprigs, for garnish (optional)

1. Trim fat from beef. Cut beef into 4 serving-size pieces. In large skillet, heat oil over medium-high heat. Cook beef pieces on both sides in hot oil until brown. Drain off fat.

2. In 3½- or 4-quart slow cooker, place onion slices. Sprinkle with tapioca, thyme, salt and pepper. Pour tomatoes over onion. Add beef.

3. Cover slow cooker; cook on low-heat setting for 10 to 12 hours or on high-heat setting for 5 to 6 hours. Serve with hot mashed potatoes. If desired, garnish with fresh thyme sprigs.

Per serving: 481 cal., 16 g total fat (5 g sat.), 89 mg chol., 1,405 mg sodium, 50 g carbo., 4 g fiber, 31 g pro.

Cheeseburger Pie

Skip the drive-through. Assemble this dish before you leave for Saturday soccer games and errands, then come home to a kid-friendly dinner and a house that smells positively yummy.

PREP: 25 minutes
COOK: 4½ to 5 hours on low-heat setting
MAKES: 6 servings

1	package (20 ounces) refrigerated mashed potatoes (2⅔ cups)
1	teaspoon dried oregano
¼	teaspoon garlic salt
2	pounds lean ground beef
2	medium-size onions, chopped
½	medium-size green pepper, seeded and chopped
2	cloves garlic, finely chopped
2	cans (14½ ounces each) Italian-style stewed tomatoes
1	can (10¾ ounces) condensed Cheddar cheese soup
½	cup shredded Cheddar cheese (2 ounces)

1. In medium-size bowl, mix together mashed potatoes, oregano and garlic salt.

2. In large skillet, cook ground beef, onion, green pepper and garlic until beef is brown and vegetables are tender, stirring occasionally. Drain off fat. Stir in tomatoes and soup.

3. Transfer beef mixture to 3½- or 4-quart slow cooker. Spoon mashed potato mixture into mounds on top of beef mixture.

4. Cover slow cooker; cook on low-heat setting for 4½ to 5 hours. Sprinkle with Cheddar cheese.

Per serving: 467 cal., 23 g total fat (9 g sat.), 112 mg chol., 990 mg sodium, 30 g carbo., 3 g fiber, 35 g pro.

Meatball Cassoulet

Cassoulet is a long-cooking rustic casserole from southwest France that features white beans, sausage and a variety of meats. This simplified version relies on work-saving frozen meatballs and smoked turkey sausage.

PREP: 25 minutes
COOK: 8 to 9 hours on low-heat setting or 4 to 4½ hours on high-heat setting
MAKES: 4 or 5 servings

2	cans (15 ounces each) Great Northern beans, drained and rinsed
2	cups tomato juice
1	package (12 ounces) frozen cooked Italian meatballs, thawed
½	pound cooked smoked turkey sausage or Polish sausage, halved lengthwise and sliced
4	medium-size carrots, peeled and finely chopped
2	ribs celery, chopped
2	medium-size onions, chopped
1	tablespoon Worcestershire sauce
½	teaspoon dried basil
½	teaspoon dried oregano
½	teaspoon paprika

1. In 3½- or 4-quart slow cooker, combine beans, tomato juice, meatballs, sausage, carrots, celery, onion, Worcestershire sauce, basil, oregano and paprika.

2. Cover slow cooker; cook on low-heat setting for 8 to 9 hours or on high-heat setting for 4 to 4½ hours.

3. To serve, ladle stew into warm bowls.

Per serving: 657 cal., 25 g total fat (11 g sat.), 93 mg chol., 1,655 mg sodium, 68 g carbo., 17 g fiber, 42 g pro.

Beef Stew with Red Wine Gravy

A Jerusalem artichoke is a root vegetable that looks like ginger but is really more like a potato. It has a slightly sweet, delicate, nutlike flavor—similar to jicama or water chestnuts.

PREP: 30 minutes
COOK: 12 to 14 hours on low-heat setting or
6 to 7 hours on high-heat setting
MAKES: 6 servings

1	boneless beef chuck roast (2 pounds)
¼	cup all-purpose flour
2	teaspoons Italian seasoning
1	teaspoon salt*
½	teaspoon black pepper
2	tablespoons olive oil
2	large onions, cut into thin wedges
½	pound parsnips, quartered lengthwise and halved
½	pound carrots, quartered lengthwise and halved
½	pound Jerusalem artichokes, peeled and coarsely chopped
1	cup dry red wine or beef broth
½	cup beef broth
¼	cup tomato paste
	Chopped plum tomatoes, golden raisins and/or red-wine vinegar or balsamic vinegar
	Crusty bread, for serving

1. Trim fat from beef. Cut beef into 1-inch cubes. In a large plastic food storage bag, combine flour, Italian seasoning, salt and pepper. Add beef to bag. Seal and gently toss to coat beef with flour mixture. In large skillet, heat oil over medium-high heat. Cook beef, half at a time, in hot oil until brown, adding more oil if necessary.

2. In 4½- to 6-quart slow cooker, combine onions, parsnips, carrots and Jerusalem artichokes. Place beef on vegetables. In small bowl, combine wine and beef broth; pour over beef.

3. Cover slow cooker; cook on low-heat setting for 12 to 14 hours or on high-heat setting for 6 to 7 hours.

4. Stir tomato paste into beef mixture. To serve, ladle stew into bowls. Pass tomatoes, raisins and/or vinegar to sprinkle on top of each serving. Serve with crusty bread.

*Note: If using all beef broth (no wine), decrease salt to ½ teaspoon.

Per serving: 356 cal., 9 g total fat (2 g sat.), 90 mg chol., 601 mg sodium, 26 g carbo., 4 g fiber, 35 g pro.

Orange-Spiced Corned Beef

A sweet, nicely spiced sauce makes a delicious contrast to the rich, salty flavor of this brisket.

PREP: 15 minutes
COOK: 8 to 10 hours on low-heat setting or
4 to 5 hours on high-heat setting
MAKES: 6 servings

1	corned beef brisket (2½ to 3 pounds)
1	package (7 ounces) mixed dried fruit
½	cup dried cranberries
2	tablespoons quick-cooking tapioca
½	cup orange juice
½	cup water
1	tablespoon mild molasses
¼	teaspoon ground cinnamon
⅛	teaspoon ground nutmeg

1. Trim fat from brisket. If necessary, cut brisket to fit into 3½- or 4-quart slow cooker. If a seasoning packet is present, discard it. Place brisket in cooker.

2. Cut any large pieces of dried fruit into quarters. Sprinkle mixed dried fruit, dried cranberries and tapioca over brisket in cooker. In small bowl, combine orange juice, water, molasses, cinnamon and nutmeg. Pour over mixture in cooker.

3. Cover slow cooker; cook on low-heat setting for 8 to 10 hours or on high-heat setting for 4 to 5 hours.

4. Remove brisket from cooker. Thinly slice meat across the grain. Arrange slices on a serving platter. Spoon fruit mixture over brisket.

Per serving: 617 cal., 36 g total fat (12 g sat.), 185 mg chol., 2,151 mg sodium, 38 g carbo., 2 g fiber, 35 g pro.

Potato, Sauerkraut and Sausage Supper

Potato, Sauerkraut and Sausage Supper

Serve this German-style dish with hearty dark rye bread, a selection of mustards, cornichons (sweet little pickles) and, if you like, cold beer.

PREP: 20 minutes
COOK: 5 to 6 hours on low-heat setting or 2½ to 3 hours on high-heat setting, plus 30 minutes on high-heat setting
MAKES: 8 servings

1	package (20 ounces) refrigerated diced potatoes with onions
2	medium-size carrots, peeled and chopped
1	large green pepper, seeded and chopped
1½	pounds cooked smoked Polish sausage, cut into 2-inch pieces
⅔	cup apple juice or apple cider
1	tablespoon cider vinegar
½	teaspoon caraway seeds
¼	teaspoon salt
¼	teaspoon black pepper
1	can (14 to 16 ounces) sauerkraut, drained

1. In 4½- to 5½-quart slow cooker, combine potatoes, carrots and green pepper. Add sausage.

2. In small bowl, combine apple juice, cider vinegar, caraway seeds, salt and black pepper. Pour over vegetable mixture in cooker.

3. Cover slow cooker; cook on low-heat setting for 5 to 6 hours or on high-heat setting for 2½ to 3 hours. If using low-heat setting, turn to high-heat setting. Stir in sauerkraut. Cover and cook for 30 minutes. To serve, transfer sausage mixture to a serving dish.

Per serving: 374 cal., 25 g total fat (9 g sat.), 60 mg chol., 1,291 mg sodium, 24 g carbo., 4 g fiber, 14 g pro.

New Potatoes and Ham

Serve this old-fashioned comfort food with a side of buttered baby sweet peas.

PREP: 20 minutes
COOK: 6 to 8 hours on low-heat setting or 3 to 4 hours on high-heat setting, plus 20 minutes on high-heat setting
MAKES: 6 servings

2	pounds tiny new potatoes, halved
4½	cups cubed cooked ham (1½ pounds)
1	teaspoon dried dill
¼	teaspoon black pepper
1	can (10½ ounces) condensed French onion soup
1	cup water
1	cup sour cream
¼	cup all-purpose flour

1. In 3½- or 4-quart slow cooker, layer potatoes and ham; sprinkle with dill and pepper. Pour onion soup and water over mixture in cooker.

2. Cover slow cooker; cook on low-heat setting for 6 to 8 hours or on high-heat setting for 3 to 4 hours.

3. In small bowl, combine sour cream and flour. Gradually stir about 1 cup of the hot cooking liquid into sour cream mixture. Add sour cream mixture to cooker, stirring gently until combined.

4. If using low-heat setting, turn to high-heat setting. Cover and cook for 20 to 30 minutes or until mixture is slightly thickened and bubbly around edges.

Per serving: 447 cal., 21 g total fat (9 g sat.), 82 mg chol., 1,940 mg sodium, 38 g carbo., 3 g fiber, 26 g pro.

Pork Lo Mein

"Lo mein" refers to the type of Chinese noodle that's traditionally used in this dish, but other kinds of noodle—such as angel hair pasta or vermicelli—make a perfectly good substitute.

PREP: 20 minutes
COOK: 6½ to 7 hours on low-heat setting or
3½ to 4 hours on high-heat setting,
plus 10 minutes on high-heat setting
MAKES: 6 servings

1	boneless pork shoulder roast (1½ pounds)
2	medium-size onions, cut into wedges
2	cups frozen sliced carrots
1	jar (12 ounces) teriyaki glaze
1	cup thinly bias-sliced celery
1	can (8 ounces) sliced water chestnuts, drained
1	can (5 ounces) sliced bamboo shoots, drained
1	teaspoon grated fresh ginger
1	package (6 ounces) frozen snow pea pods
1	cup broccoli flowerets
9	ounces curly, thin egg noodles
¼	cup cashews

1. Trim fat from pork. Cut pork into ¾-inch pieces. In 3½- or 4-quart slow cooker, combine pork, onions, carrots, teriyaki glaze, celery, water chestnuts, bamboo shoots and ginger.

2. Cover slow cooker; cook on low-heat setting for 6½ to 7 hours or on high-heat setting for 3½ to 4 hours.

3. If using low-heat setting, turn to high-heat setting. Stir in frozen pea pods and broccoli. Cover and cook for 10 to 15 minutes or until pea pods are crisp-tender.

4. Cook noodles following package directions. Drain well. To serve, spoon pork mixture over noodles. Sprinkle each serving with cashews.

Per serving: 509 cal., 12 g total fat (3 g sat.), 73 mg chol., 2,274 mg sodium, 66 g carbo., 6 g fiber, 33 g pro.

Drumsticks with Barbecue Sauce

By broiling the chicken drumsticks before you put them in the slow cooker, you get the best of both worlds: crisp, caramelized skin and falling-off-the bone tenderness.

PREP: 15 minutes
COOK: 3 to 4 hours on low-heat setting or
1½ to 2 hours on high-heat setting
BROIL: 15 to 20 minutes
MAKES: 8 servings

3	**pounds chicken drumsticks**
1½	**cups bottled barbecue sauce**
¼	**cup honey**
2	**teaspoons yellow mustard**
1½	**teaspoons Worcestershire sauce**

1. Heat broiler. Place chicken on unheated rack of broiler pan. Broil 4 to 5 inches from heat for 15 to 20 minutes or until light brown, turning once. In 3½- or 4-quart slow cooker, place chicken.

2. In medium-size bowl, combine barbecue sauce, honey, mustard and Worcestershire sauce. Pour over chicken.

3. Cover slow cooker; cook on low-heat setting for 3 to 4 hours or on high-heat setting for 1½ to 2 hours.

Per serving: 83 cal., 4 g total fat (1 g sat.), 20 mg chol., 197 mg sodium, 6 g carbo., 0 g fiber, 5 g pro.

Chicken Enchilada Casserole

PREP: 15 minutes
COOK: 5 hours on low-heat setting or
2½ hours on high-heat setting
STAND: 15 minutes
MAKES: 8 servings

9	(6-inch) corn tortillas
1	can (11 ounces) whole kernel corn with sweet red peppers, drained
1	package (6 ounces) refrigerated cooked Southwestern-flavored chicken breast strips, cut up
1	can (4 ounces) diced green chiles, undrained
2	cups shredded Mexican-blend cheese (8 ounces)
1	can (19 ounces) enchilada sauce
1	can (15 ounces) black beans, drained
1	carton (6 ounces) frozen avocado dip (guacamole), thawed, for serving
½	cup sour cream, for serving

1. Lightly coat 3½- or 4-quart slow cooker with nonstick cooking spray. Place 3 of the tortillas in bottom of prepared cooker, overlapping as necessary. Top with corn, half of the chicken and half of the green chiles; sprinkle with ½ cup of the cheese. Pour about ¾ cup of the enchilada sauce over mixture in cooker. Repeat with 3 more tortillas, the black beans, remaining chicken and remaining green chiles; sprinkle with another ½ cup of the cheese. Pour another ¾ cup of the enchilada sauce over mixture. Top with remaining 3 tortillas, remaining 1 cup cheese and remaining enchilada sauce.

2. Cover slow cooker; cook on low-heat setting for 5 hours or on high-heat setting for 2½ hours. Remove liner from cooker, if possible, or turn off cooker. Cover and let stand for 15 minutes. Serve with avocado dip and sour cream.

Per serving: 368 cal., 18 g total fat (7 g sat.), 44 mg chol., 1,031 mg sodium, 39 g carbo., 6 g fiber, 18 g pro.

Angel Chicken

The fresh chives are optional, but they really do add bright green color and fresh flavor to the finished dish.

PREP: 15 minutes
COOK: 4 to 5 hours on low-heat setting
MAKES: 4 servings

1	package (8 ounces) fresh button mushrooms, quartered
1	package (6 ounces) fresh shiitake mushrooms, stems removed, caps sliced
4	boneless, skinless chicken breast halves (about 1½ pounds)
4	tablespoons (½ stick) butter
1	packet (0.7 ounce) dry Italian salad dressing mix
1	can (10¾ ounces) condensed golden mushroom soup
½	cup dry white wine
½	tub (8 ounces) cream cheese spread with chives and onion
	Hot cooked angel hair pasta or hot cooked rice
	Chopped fresh chives (optional)

1. In 3½- or 4-quart slow cooker, place the mushrooms; top with chicken breasts. In medium-size saucepan, melt butter over medium heat; stir in Italian dressing mix, mushroom soup, white wine and cream cheese. Stir until cheese melts; pour over chicken.

2. Cover slow cooker; cook on low-heat setting for 4 to 5 hours.

3. Serve chicken and sauce over cooked pasta or rice. If desired, sprinkle with chives.

Per serving: 405 cal., 17 g total fat (9 g sat.), 110 mg chol., 1,043 mg sodium, 26 g carbo., 1 g fiber, 32 g pro.

Angel Chicken

Pioneer Beans

This hearty version of baked beans gets a flavor boost from the addition of ground beef and bacon.

PREP: 15 minutes
COOK: 5 to 6 hours on low-heat setting or 2½ to 3 hours on high-heat setting
MAKES: 12 side-dish servings

1	pound lean ground beef
4	strips bacon, chopped
1	medium-size onion, chopped
1	can (15 ounces) red kidney beans, drained
1	can (15 ounces) butter beans, drained
1	can (15 ounces) pork and beans in tomato sauce
1	cup ketchup
½	to 1 cup packed light-brown sugar
¼	cup molasses
1	tablespoon vinegar
1	tablespoon yellow mustard

1. In large skillet, cook beef, bacon and onion over medium heat until beef is brown and onion is tender. Drain off fat.

2. In 3½- or 4-quart slow cooker, combine ground beef mixture, kidney beans, butter beans, pork and beans, ketchup, brown sugar, molasses, vinegar and mustard.

3. Cover slow cooker; cook on low-heat setting for 5 to 6 hours or on high-heat setting for 2½ to 3 hours.

Per serving: 256 cal., 7 g total fat (2 g sat.), 28 mg chol., 684 mg sodium, 38 g carbo., 4 g fiber, 15 g pro.

Easy Cheesy Potatoes

These potatoes are wickedly good. Take them to a potluck and they disappear before anything else (even the desserts). Pictured on page 69.

PREP: 15 minutes
COOK: 5 to 6 hours on low-heat setting
MAKES: 12 side-dish servings

1	package (28 ounces) frozen diced hash brown potatoes with onion and peppers, thawed
1	can (10¾ ounces) condensed cream of chicken with herbs soup
1	cup finely shredded smoked Gouda cheese (4 ounces)
1	cup finely shredded provolone cheese (4 ounces)
1	package (8 ounces) cream cheese, cut into cubes
¾	cup milk
¼	cup sliced leek or thinly sliced scallions
½	teaspoon black pepper
4	strips bacon, crisp-cooked and crumbled

1. In 3½- or 4-quart slow cooker, combine potatoes, soup, Gouda cheese, provolone cheese, cream cheese, milk, leek and black pepper.

2. Cover slow cooker; cook on low-heat setting for 5 to 6 hours. Sprinkle with bacon before serving.

Per serving: 218 cal., 14 g total fat (8 g sat.), 41 mg chol., 564 mg sodium, 16 g carbo., 2 g fiber, 9 g pro.

Three Sisters Corn-Chili Chowder

The "sisters" in the title of this recipe refers to its use of the three of Native American cooking: corn, beans and squash.

PREP: 25 minutes
COOK: 8 to 9 hours on low-heat setting or
4 to 4½ hours on high-heat setting, plus
30 minutes on high-heat setting
MAKES: 6 to 8 servings

3	large red-skin potatoes, peeled if desired and cut into ½-inch cubes (about 1½ pounds)
1½	cups frozen corn
1	cup frozen baby lima beans
1	medium-size onion, chopped
½	cup chopped fresh Anaheim or poblano chiles* or green pepper
½	medium-size sweet red pepper, seeded and chopped
1	can (4 ounces) diced green chiles, drained
3	cloves garlic, minced
½	teaspoon salt
2	cans (14 ounces each) vegetable broth
1	can (14¾ ounces) cream-style corn
1	small zucchini, halved lengthwise and sliced crosswise
1	cup heavy cream

1. In 4- to 6-quart slow cooker, combine potatoes, frozen corn, frozen lima beans, onion, fresh chiles, red pepper, canned chiles, garlic and salt. Pour broth over all.

2. Cover slow cooker; cook on low-heat setting for 8 to 9 hours or on high-heat setting for 4 to 4½ hours.

3. If using low-heat setting, turn to high-heat setting. Stir in corn and zucchini. Cover and cook for 30 minutes. Stir in cream.

4. To serve, ladle chowder into bowls.

*Note: Anaheim and other hot chiles contain oils that can burn your skin and eyes. Avoid direct contact with them as much as possible. When working with hot chiles, wear plastic or rubber gloves. If your bare hands do touch the chiles, wash your hands well with soap and warm water.

Per serving: 383 cal., 17 g total fat (9 g sat.), 55 mg chol., 1,073 mg sodium, 54 g carbo., 6 g fiber, 10 g pro.

Chapter 5

Get Fired Up

Great Grilling

Put some sizzle in your supper with these flame-kissed recipes for your preferred meat, poultry and fish. Where there is smoke and fire, there is fabulous flavor.

Sticky Sloppy Barbecue Chicken

Polish Sausage Foil Dinner

Polish Sausage Foil Dinner

When you dine in the great outdoors, you want something hearty, heartwarming and easy to make. Former Girl Scout leader Joyce Andrews of Pittsburgh developed this recipe for her family. It became one of Troop 83's favorite camping dinners. The troop included it in its 1999 cookbook, *A Taste of the Outdoors*, now in its 20th printing!

PREP: 5 minutes
GRILL: 15 minutes
STAND: 5 minutes
MAKES: 1 serving

1   cup frozen diced hash brown potatoes with onion and peppers, thawed
3   ounces smoked sausage, sliced crosswise to, but not through
1   tablespoon bottled Italian salad dressing
2   tablespoons shredded Cheddar cheese

1. Fold 24×12-inch piece of heavy foil in half to create a square. Place potatoes and sausage in center of foil. Drizzle Italian salad dressing over potatoes and sausage. Bring together two opposite edges of foil and seal with a double fold. Fold remaining edges together to completely enclose mixture, leaving space for steam to build.

2. Heat gas grill to medium or prepare charcoal grill with medium coals. Grill foil packet about 15 minutes or until potatoes are tender and sausage is heated through, turning once.

3. To serve, carefully open packet. Sprinkle potato and sausage mixture with cheese. Reseal packet; let stand about 5 minutes or until cheese melts.

Per serving: 557 cal., 40 g total fat (14 g sat.), 73 mg chol., 1,499 mg sodium, 29 g carbo., 0 g fiber, 25 g pro.

Rick's Beef Brisket

Most people who see the "Smokin' Salmons" sign on top of the big black smoker at barbecue contests think they're going to get a taste of some good smoked fish. And sometimes they do. But most of the time, Rick Salmon and his barbecue buddies, Steve and Stu, are cooking up something a bit more traditional—like saucy, slow-smoked brisket.

SOAK: 1 hour
PREP: 20 minutes
SMOKE: 2 to 2½ hours
MAKES: 15 servings

4   **cups mesquite or hickory wood chips**
Rub:
2   **tablespoons sugar**
1   **tablespoon garlic salt or seasoned salt**
1   **tablespoon paprika**
1½   **teaspoons chili powder**
1½   **teaspoons black pepper**
⅛   **teaspoon ground red pepper**
⅛   **teaspoon celery seeds**
        Pinch of ground cloves
Mop (sauce):
½   **cup beer**
1   **tablespoon cider vinegar**
1   **tablespoon olive oil**
1   **tablespoon Worcestershire sauce**
1   **tablespoon bottled barbecue sauce**
½   **teaspoon seasoned salt**
¼   **teaspoon celery seeds**
Brisket:
1   **fresh beef brisket (3 to 4 pounds)**

1. At least 1 hour before cooking, soak wood chips or chunks in enough water to cover. Drain before using.

2. Rub: Combine sugar, garlic salt, paprika, chili powder, black pepper, red pepper, the ⅛ teaspoon celery seeds and cloves. Set aside.

3. Mop (sauce): In another small bowl, combine beer, vinegar, oil, Worcestershire sauce, barbecue sauce, ½ teaspoon seasoned salt and ¼ teaspoon celery seeds. Set aside.

4. Trim fat from meat. Sprinkle rub over meat; pat in. Place meat on grill rack over a drip pan. (For gas grill, place meat on a rack in a roaster pan.) Smoke 2 to 2½ hours on covered grill.* Brush once or twice with Mop sauce during last hour of cooking.

***Smoking Basics:** In a charcoal grill, arrange medium-hot coals around a drip pan. Test for medium heat above the pan. Sprinkle soaked and drained wood chips over coals. Place meat on the grill rack over drip pan. Cover and smoke as directed in recipe. In a gas grill, preheat grill. Reduce heat to medium. Adjust for indirect cooking. Add drained wood chips according to manufacturer's directions. Place meat on rack over drip pan. Cover; smoke as directed in recipe.

Per serving: 262 cal., 20 g total fat (7 g sat.), 61 mg chol., 436 mg sodium, 3 g carbo., 0 g fiber, 16 g pro.

Rick's Beef Brisket

Grilled Southwestern Salmon Salad

Edwina Gadsby of St. Simons, Georgia, knows that mild-tasting salmon soaks up all kinds of wonderful flavors. The California native gravitated toward a Mexican twist when she developed this fabulously fresh main-dish salad recipe. It garnered her the $1,000 prize in a National Fisheries Institute Contest.

PREP: 20 minutes
MARINATE: 1 to 2 hours
GRILL: 8 to 12 minutes
MAKES: 4 servings

½	cup orange juice
⅓	cup lime juice
¼	cup dry sherry
½	cup chopped fresh cilantro leaves
1	tablespoon finely chopped chipotle pepper in adobo sauce*
2	tablespoons honey
½	teaspoon salt
¼	teaspoon black pepper
¼	cup vegetable oil
4	salmon fillets (6 ounces each, 1 inch thick)
6	cups torn mixed salad greens
2	cups chopped ripe mango (2 to 3 medium-size)
1	large sweet red pepper, seeded and cut into thin strips
1	small red onion, halved lengthwise and thinly sliced

1. In small bowl, combine orange juice, lime juice, sherry, cilantro, chipotle pepper, honey, half of the salt and half of the black pepper. Divide in half; whisk oil into half of the mixture for dressing.

2. In large plastic food-storage bag, combine salmon and remaining juice mixture. Seal bag. Marinate in refrigerator for 1 to 2 hours, turning bag often. Remove salmon from marinade; sprinkle with remaining salt and pepper. Discard marinade.

3. Heat gas grill to medium or prepare charcoal grill with medium coals. Grill fish, skin side up, for 8 to 12 minutes or until fish flakes when tested. Remove skin from fish. Combine greens, mango, sweet pepper, onion and reserved dressing mixture. Divide evenly among dinner plates. Top with a salmon fillet.

*Note: Hot chiles contain volatile oils that can burn your skin and eyes. Avoid direct contact with them as much as possible. When working with hot chiles, wear plastic or rubber gloves. If your bare hands do touch the chiles, wash your hands well with soap and warm water.

Per serving: 352 cal., 18 g total fat (5 g sat.), 56 mg chol., 588 mg sodium, 27 g carbo., 2 g fiber, 5 g pro.

Grilled Southwestern Salmon Salad

Grilled Sweet and Hot Alaskan Shrimp

Grilled Sweet and Hot Alaskan Shrimp

Be careful not to exceed the 3-hour marinating time. As it soaks, the shrimp "cooks" in the acidic lime juice and starts to break down—and you don't want it getting mushy and falling apart on the grill!

PREP: 30 minutes
MARINATE: 2 to 3 hours
GRILL: 8 to 10 minutes
MAKES: 4 servings

1	pound jumbo shrimp in shells
½	cup orange marmalade
⅓	cup lime juice
3	tablespoons chopped fresh cilantro leaves
1	fresh jalapeño chile, seeded and chopped*
2	teaspoons dark Asian sesame oil
½	teaspoon seasoned salt
4	strips bacon
	Hot cooked rice, for serving (optional)
	Thinly sliced oranges and limes, for garnish (optional)

1. Peel and devein shrimp, leaving tails intact. Rinse shrimp and pat dry. Combine marmalade, lime juice, cilantro, jalapeño chile, sesame oil and seasoned salt. Cook and stir over medium heat until marmalade is melted. Remove from heat; cool.

2. In plastic food-storage bag, combine shrimp and cooled marinade. Seal bag. Refrigerate for 2 to 3 hours. Drain shrimp; discard marinade.

3. In medium-size skillet, cook bacon over medium heat for 4 to 5 minutes or until almost cooked through but still pliable. Cool bacon on paper towels. Using kitchen shears, cut each slice of bacon crosswise into quarters. On four long metal skewers, starting with bacon, alternately thread 4 bacon pieces and 4 shrimp onto each skewer.

4. Heat gas grill to medium-low or prepare charcoal grill with medium-low coals. Grill skewers for 8 to 10 minutes or until shrimp turn pink and are cooked through. Turn skewers every 2 minutes to prevent bacon from sticking. If desired, serve skewers over hot cooked rice and garnish with orange and lime.

***Note:** Hot chiles contain oils that can burn your skin and eyes. Avoid direct contact with them as much as possible. When working with hot chiles, wear plastic or rubber gloves. If your bare hands do touch the chiles, wash your hands well with soap and warm water.

Per serving: 165 cal., 5 g total fat (1 g sat.), 138 mg chol., 364 mg sodium, 8 g carbo., 0 g fiber, 20 g pro.

Cheese-Topped Steaks

Coarse salt has more flavor than regular salt, and the grains look pretty on the grilled crust of these juicy steaks. Look for it in the spice aisle of your grocery store.

PREP: 20 minutes
GRILL: 11 to 14 minutes
MAKES: 4 servings

½	cup **Gorgonzola cheese or other blue cheese, crumbled (2 ounces)**
¼	cup **cooked bacon pieces**
¼	cup **pine nuts or slivered almonds, toasted**
2	tablespoons **chopped fresh thyme leaves**
2	cloves **garlic, finely chopped**
¼	teaspoon **black pepper**
	Coarse salt or salt
4	**boneless beef top loin steaks, cut 1 inch thick (about 3 pounds total)**

1. In small bowl, combine cheese, bacon, nuts, thyme, garlic and pepper; set aside.

2. Sprinkle steaks lightly with salt. Heat gas grill to medium or prepare charcoal grill with medium coals. Grill steaks for 10 to 12 minutes or until internal temperature registers 145° (medium rare) on an instant-read meat thermometer inserted in center of steaks. Turn steaks over once, halfway through grilling.

3. To serve, top steaks with cheese mixture. Grill for 1 to 2 minutes more to soften cheese slightly.

Per serving: 640 cal., 30 g total fat (11 g sat.), 181 mg chol., 616 mg sodium, 3 g carbo., 0 g fiber, 86 g pro.

Caesar Salad Burgers

A generous amount of garlic, plus romaine lettuce and Parmesan cheese—all components of classic Caesar salad— inspired the creation of these tasty burgers. Drizzle a little Caesar dressing on the burgers before topping them with the toasted bread, if you like.

PREP: 15 minutes
GRILL: 13 to 15 minutes
MAKES: 4 servings

1½	pounds ground beef
1	teaspoon salt
½	teaspoon black pepper
3	cloves garlic, finely chopped
8	slices sourdough bread
	Olive oil
2	large cloves garlic, cut lengthwise into quarters
4	romaine lettuce leaves
¼	cup shredded Parmesan cheese

1. In large bowl, mix together beef, salt, pepper and the finely chopped garlic. Form into four ¾-inch-thick patties, shaping to fit bread.

2. Heat gas grill to medium or prepare charcoal grill with medium coals. Grill burgers for 13 to 15 minutes or until internal temperature registers 160° on an instant-read thermometer inserted in centers of burgers. Turn burgers once halfway through grilling.

3. Brush both sides of bread with oil. Place bread around outer edge of grill. Grill a few minutes until lightly toasted, turning once; remove from grill. Rub both sides of each slice with a garlic quarter.

4. To serve, place a lettuce leaf and a burger on 4 bread slices; sprinkle with cheese. Cover with remaining 4 bread slices.

Per serving: 481 cal., 23 g total fat (7 g sat.), 112 mg chol., 984 mg sodium, 28 g carbo., 1 g fiber, 38 g pro.

Texas Hill Country T-Bones

PREP: 20 minutes
CHILL: salsa up to 24 hours
GRILL: 26 to 30 minutes
MAKES: 4 servings

Salsa:

1	medium-size sweet red pepper, seeded and finely chopped
½	cup finely chopped papaya
½	cup chopped fresh cilantro leaves
¼	cup finely chopped jicama
2	tablespoons lime juice
1	small fresh habañero chile, seeded and finely chopped
1	tablespoon honey (optional)

Onions and Steaks:

2	medium-size red onions, halved lengthwise and very thinly sliced
4	beef T-bone steaks (8 ounces each, cut 1 inch thick)
⅓	cup chopped fresh sage leaves or 4 teaspoons dried sage
1½	teaspoons coarse salt
1½	teaspoons ground cumin
1	teaspoon red pepper flakes

1. Salsa: Combine red pepper, papaya, cilantro, jicama, lime juice, chile, honey (if desired) and ¼ teaspoon salt. Cover; refrigerate up to 24 hours.

2. Onions and Steaks: Heat gas grill to medium or prepare charcoal grill with medium coals. Place onions in a grill basket. Grill 15 minutes or until brown and crisp, rearranging and turning once. Remove onions. Meanwhile, trim fat from steaks. Combine sage, coarse salt, cumin and pepper flakes. Sprinkle over both sides of steaks; pat in.

3. Grill steaks 11 to 15 minutes or until internal temperature registers 145° (medium rare) on an instant-read meat thermometer inserted in center of steaks. Serve with grilled onions and salsa.

Per serving: 375 cal., 14 g total fat (4 g sat.), 108 mg chol., 993 mg sodium, 12 g carbo., 3 g fiber, 49 g pro.

Garlic-Chili-Rubbed Lamb Chops

PREP: 15 minutes
MARINATE: 4 to 24 hours
GRILL: 16 to 18 minutes
MAKES: 4 servings

Garlic-Chili Rub:
4	large cloves garlic, finely chopped
½	teaspoon salt
1	tablespoon chili powder
1	teaspoon ground cumin
½	teaspoon sugar
½	teaspoon black pepper
½	teaspoon dried thyme
¼	teaspoon ground cinnamon
¼	teaspoon ground allspice
2	to 3 teaspoons olive oil

Lamb Chops:
8	lamb rib or loin chops, cut 1 inch thick

1. Garlic-Chili Rub: On cutting board, with the flat side of a chef's knife, mash together garlic and salt until a paste forms. Transfer garlic paste to small bowl. Stir in chili powder, cumin, sugar, pepper, thyme, cinnamon and allspice. Stir in enough of the olive oil to make a paste.

2. Lamb Chops: Rub paste over all sides of lamb chops. Cover lamb; refrigerate for 4 to 24 hours.

3. Heat gas grill to medium-high; reduce heat to medium and adjust for indirect cooking. Or prepare charcoal grill with medium-hot coals; arrange coals around a drip pan. Test for medium heat above drip pan. Place chops on grill rack over drip pan. Cover and grill for 16 to 18 minutes or until internal temperature registers 145° (medium rare) on an instant-read meat thermometer inserted in center of chops.

Per serving: 223 cal., 14 g total fat (4 g sat.), 64 mg chol., 383 mg sodium, 3 g carbo., 1 g fiber, 20 g pro.

Basil-Buttered Steak and Potatoes

PREP: 20 minutes
GRILL: potatoes about 35 minutes; steak 14 to 18 minutes
MAKES: 4 servings

Potato Packet:
4	tablespoons (½ stick) butter, softened
¼	cup chopped fresh basil leaves
1	teaspoon lemon-pepper seasoning
2	cloves garlic, finely chopped
3	medium-size red- and/or yellow-skin potatoes, cut into ¼-inch-thick slices
2	medium-size red and/or yellow onions, thinly sliced and separated into rings

Steak:
1	boneless beef sirloin steak, cut 1 inch thick (1 pound)

1. Potato Packet: Fold 36×18-inch piece of heavy foil in half to make 18-inch square. Combine butter, basil, lemon-pepper seasoning and garlic. Set aside one-fourth of the basil-butter mixture. Place potatoes and onions in center of foil; dot with remaining basil-butter mixture. Bring together two opposite edges of foil; seal with a double fold. Fold remaining edges to enclose vegetables, leaving space for steam to build. Heat gas grill to medium-high or prepare charcoal grill with medium-hot coals. Grill packet about 35 minutes or until potatoes are tender.

2. Steak: Trim fat from steak. Add steak to grill for the last 14 to 18 minutes of grilling or until internal temperature registers 145° (medium rare) on an instant-read meat thermometer inserted in center of steak. Turn steak once halfway through. Transfer steak to platter; dot with reserved basil-butter mixture. Slice steak across the grain; season to taste with salt and black pepper. Serve with potatoes and onions. If desired, garnish with basil.

Per serving: 350 cal., 16 g total fat (9 g sat.), 91 mg chol., 574 mg sodium, 22 g carbo., 3 g fiber, 28 g pro.

Basil-Buttered Steak and Potatoes

Pork Pocket Delight

When you bite into these juicy pork chops, you get a creamy, melty mouthful of cumin-infused cream cheese.

PREP: 20 minutes
GRILL: 35 to 40 minutes
MAKES: 4 servings

6	ounces cream cheese, softened
1	teaspoon ground cumin
4	pork loin or rib chops, cut 1 to 1¼ inches thick
	Salt
	Black pepper
⅔	cup apricot preserves
¼	cup dried cranberries
2	tablespoons horseradish

1. In small bowl, soak 8 wooden picks in water for 10 minutes. In another small bowl, stir together cream cheese and cumin. Make a pocket in each chop by cutting horizontally from outside edge almost to the bone. Spoon one-fourth of the cream cheese mixture into pocket of each chop. Secure openings with wooden picks. Season chops with salt and pepper.

2. Heat gas grill to medium-high; adjust for indirect cooking. Or prepare charcoal grill with medium-hot coals; arrange coals around drip pan. Test for medium heat above drip pan. Arrange chops on grill rack over drip pan. Cover and grill for 35 to 40 minutes or until internal temperature registers 160° on an instant-read meat thermometer inserted in center of chops. Turn chops once halfway through grilling.

3. In small saucepan, combine preserves, cranberries and horseradish. During last 5 minutes of grilling, place pan over heat on outside edge of grill. To serve, spoon some glaze over chops. Pass remaining glaze.

Per serving: 607 cal., 25 g total fat (13 g sat.), 152 mg chol., 393 mg sodium, 45 g carbo., 1 g fiber, 46 g pro.

Jamaican Jerk Pork Loin

You have to plan ahead a little bit to make this recipe—the pork bathes in a sweet and spicy rum-spiked brine overnight before it's grilled—but it's well worth the effort. Brining the pork flavors it and makes it butter-knife tender.

PREP: 25 minutes
MARINATE: 12 to 14 hours
GRILL: 1 to 1¼ hours
STAND: 10 minutes
MAKES: 8 servings

Brine and Pork:
- 4 cups unsweetened pineapple juice
- ⅓ cup coarse kosher salt
- ¼ cup packed light-brown sugar
- ¼ cup rum
- 2 tablespoons jerk seasoning
- 1 boneless pork top loin roast (2 to 2½ pounds)

Mint-Pineapple Salsa:
- 2 tablespoons jalapeño pepper jelly
- 1 cup chopped fresh pineapple
- ½ cup chopped mango or papaya
- ¼ cup chopped star fruit
- 2 scallions, trimmed and thinly sliced
- 2 tablespoons chopped fresh mint leaves

1. Brine and Pork: In stainless-steel or enamel pot, or in plastic container large enough to hold roast, combine pineapple juice, salt, brown sugar, rum and jerk seasoning. Stir to dissolve salt. Carefully add pork. Cover and marinate in refrigerator for at least 12 hours or up to 14 hours, turning pork occasionally.

2. Mint-Pineapple Salsa: In medium-size microwave-safe bowl, microwave jelly on HIGH about 30 seconds or until melted. Stir in pineapple, mango, star fruit, scallions and mint. Cover and refrigerate until ready to serve.

3. Remove pork from brine; discard brine. Rinse pork and pat dry with paper towels.

4. Heat gas grill to medium-high; reduce heat to medium and adjust for indirect cooking. Or prepare charcoal grill with medium-hot coals; arrange coals around a drip pan. Test for medium heat above drip pan. Add additional coals as needed to maintain temperature. Place pork on grill rack over drip pan. Cover and grill for 1 to 1¼ hours or until internal temperature registers 155° on an instant-read meat thermometer inserted in center of pork. Remove meat from grill. Cover and let stand for 10 minutes before carving. (The roast's temperature will rise about 5° during standing.) Slice roast and serve with mint-pineapple salsa.

Per serving: 214 cal., 6 g total fat (2 g sat.), 62 mg chol., 561 mg sodium, 12 g carbo., 1 g fiber, 25 g pro.

Pork Tenderloin with Dijon Sauce

Enjoy this Chinese-style pork dish with a full-bodied red wine or a dark beer.

PREP: 10 minutes
CHILL: 1½ hours
GRILL: 30 to 35 minutes
STAND: 10 minutes
MAKES: 6 to 8 servings

Pork:
2	pork tenderloins (1 pound each)
½	teaspoon onion powder
⅓	cup bottled stir-fry sauce
¼	teaspoon black pepper

Dijon Sauce:
½	cup light mayonnaise
3	tablespoons bottled stir-fry sauce
2	tablespoons Dijon mustard
1	teaspoon vegetable oil

1. Pork: Sprinkle pork with onion powder; place in shallow baking dish. Pour the ⅓ cup stir-fry sauce over pork. Sprinkle with pepper. Cover; refrigerate for 1½ hours.

2. Dijon Sauce: Whisk together mayonnaise, the 3 tablespoons stir-fry sauce, mustard and oil. Cover; refrigerate until serving time.

3. Heat gas grill to medium-high; reduce heat to medium and adjust for indirect cooking. Or prepare charcoal grill with medium-hot coals; arrange coals around drip pan. Test for medium heat above drip pan. Place pork on grill rack over drip pan. Cover and grill for 30 to 35 minutes or until internal temperature registers 155° on an instant-read meat thermometer inserted in center of pork. Remove pork from grill. Cover with foil; let stand for 10 minutes before slicing. (The meat's temperature will rise about 5° during standing.) Cut meat into ½-inch-thick slices. Serve meat slices with sauce.

Per serving: 270 cal., 10 g total fat (2 g. sat), 105 mg chol., 810 mg sodium, 8 g carbo., 0 g fiber, 34 g pro.

Chicken Spiedini

PREP: 30 minutes
MARINATE: 2 to 24 hours
GRILL: 10 to 12 minutes
MAKES: 4 servings

1¼	pounds chicken breast tenderloins
⅔	cup bottled sweet Italian salad dressing
¾	cup packaged seasoned dry bread crumbs
¾	cup halved fresh mushrooms
2	cloves garlic, finely chopped
1	tablespoon butter
¼	cup coarsely chopped prosciutto
¾	cup shredded mozzarella cheese
1	lemon, quartered

1. In large plastic food-storage bag, combine chicken and salad dressing. Seal bag and turn to coat chicken. Marinate in refrigerator for 2 to 24 hours, turning bag occasionally.

2. Drain chicken; discard marinade. Dip chicken in bread crumbs to coat. On five or six long metal skewers, thread chicken, accordion-style, leaving ¼-inch space between pieces.

3. Heat gas grill to medium or prepare charcoal grill with medium coals. Grill skewers for 10 to 12 minutes or until internal temperature registers 170° on an instant-read meat thermometer. Turn skewers once halfway through grilling.

4. In large skillet, cook and stir mushrooms and garlic in hot butter 5 minutes or just until tender. Add prosciutto; cook and stir 2 minutes more.

5. Remove chicken from skewers; arrange on plates. Sprinkle chicken with half of the cheese. Spoon on mushroom mixture. Sprinkle with remaining cheese. Squeeze lemon over top.

Per serving: 471 cal., 22 g total fat (6 g sat.), 113 mg chol., 1,820 mg sodium, 22 g carbo., 0 g fiber, 46 g pro.

Chicken Spiedini

Pear and Chicken Salad

The sweetness of pears is wonderful with the sharp tanginess of blue cheese. You can use any kind of pear—Bartlett, Anjou, Bosc or Comice.

PREP: 20 minutes
GRILL: 12 to 15 minutes
MAKES: 4 servings

¾   pound fresh asparagus spears, stems and tough ends trimmed
2   small pears, halved lengthwise and cored (remove stems, if desired)
      Lemon juice
4   boneless, skinless chicken breast halves (about 1¼ pounds total)
      Salt
      Black pepper

Blue Cheese Dressing:
½   cup plain fat-free yogurt
¼   cup chopped red onion
2   tablespoons crumbled blue cheese
1   tablespoon chopped fresh chives
⅛   teaspoon white or black pepper
      Milk (optional)
6   cups torn mixed salad greens

1. If desired, scrape scales off asparagus. In large saucepan, cook asparagus, covered, in a small amount of lightly salted boiling water for 3 to 5 minutes or until crisp-tender. Drain.

2. Brush cut sides of pears with lemon juice. Season chicken with salt and pepper.

3. Heat gas grill to medium or prepare charcoal grill with medium coals. Grill chicken for 5 minutes. Turn chicken. Add pears to grill, cut sides down. Grill chicken and pears for 7 to 10 minutes more or until temperature registers 170° on an instant-read meat thermometer inserted in chicken. If desired, add asparagus for the last 3 minutes of grilling. Transfer chicken to cutting board; slice chicken. Cut pear halves in half, forming 8 wedges.

4. Blue Cheese Dressing: In small bowl, combine yogurt, onion, blue cheese, chives and pepper. If desired, stir milk into mixture to reach desired consistency.

5. To serve, on four dinner plates, arrange greens, chicken and asparagus. Spoon dressing over salads. Place 2 pear wedges on each salad.

Per serving: 245 cal., 3 g total fat (1 g sat.), 86 mg chol., 314 mg sodium, 16 g carbo., 4 g fiber, 38 g pro.

Sticky Sloppy Barbecue Chicken

Pictured on page 91.

PREP: 45 minutes
MARINATE: 2 to 4 hours
GRILL: 50 to 60 minutes
MAKES: 6 servings

Chicken and Marinade:
- 3 to 4 pounds meaty chicken pieces
- 1½ cups dry sherry
- 2 medium-size onions, finely chopped
- ¼ cup lemon juice
- 6 cloves garlic, finely chopped
- 2 bay leaves

Barbecue Sauce:
- 1 can (15 ounces) tomato puree
- ¼ cup honey
- 3 tablespoons molasses
- ½ teaspoon dried thyme
- ¼ to ½ teaspoon cayenne pepper
- ¼ teaspoon ground black pepper
- 2 tablespoons white vinegar

1. Chicken and Marinade: In food-storage bag, combine chicken, sherry, onions, lemon juice, garlic and bay leaves. Seal bag. Chill 2 to 4 hours, turning bag often. Drain chicken; reserve marinade.

2. Barbecue Sauce: Combine reserved marinade, tomatoes, honey, molasses, 1 teaspoon salt, thyme and peppers. Bring to a boil; reduce heat. Simmer until reduced to 2 cups. Discard leaves. Add vinegar.

3. Pat chicken dry. Heat gas grill to medium-high; adjust grill for indirect cooking. Or prepare charcoal grill with medium-hot coals; arrange coals around drip pan. Place chicken, bone side down, over drip pan. Cover; grill 50 to 60 minutes or until temperature registers 170° for breast halves and 180° for thighs and drumsticks. Brush with some sauce during last 15 minutes. Heat remaining sauce until bubbly; serve with chicken.

Per serving: 446 cal., 13 g total fat (4 g sat.), 104 mg chol., 735 mg sodium, 33 g carbo., 2 g fiber, 35 g pro.

Turkey Sausage with Cranberry Sauce

PREP: 20 minutes
GRILL: 15 to 18 minutes
MAKES: 6 servings

Cranberry Sauce:
- 1 can (16 ounces) whole berry cranberry sauce
- 1 tablespoon finely shredded orange peel
- ¼ cup orange juice
- 4 cloves garlic, finely chopped

Turkey Sausage:
- 1¼ pounds ground turkey
- ¼ pound ground pork sausage
- 10 cloves garlic, finely chopped
- 1 tablespoon chopped fresh marjoram leaves or 1 teaspoon dried marjoram
- 1 tablespoon chopped fresh oregano leaves or 1 teaspoon dried oregano
- 1 tablespoon chopped fresh parsley
- 1 teaspoon salt
- ¼ teaspoon black pepper
  Pinch of cayenne pepper

1. Cranberry Sauce: Combine canned sauce, orange peel, juice and 4 cloves garlic. Reserve ¼ cup sauce. Cover; chill remaining sauce.

2. Turkey Sausage: Mix meats, the 10 cloves garlic, herbs, salt, and peppers. Divide mixture into six portions. Shape each portion around a metal skewer, forming a 5-inch log.

3. Heat gas grill to medium or prepare charcoal grill with medium coals. Grill 15 to 18 minutes or until temperature registers 165° on an instant-read meat thermometer. Turn skewers to brown evenly; brush with ¼ cup reserved sauce halfway through. Serve with remaining sauce.

Per serving: 350 cal., 15 g total fat (5 g sat.), 87 mg chol., 620 mg sodium, 34 g carbo., 2 g fiber, 19 g pro.

Chapter 6

Good For You

Healthy Favorites

Great-tasting food can be healthful and satisfying. These luscious dishes are low in fat and calories and loaded with fruits and vegetables.

Ziti with Ricotta and Vegetables

Hearty Mushroom and Beef Soup

Step into the kitchen of Pam D'Alessandro, of Pittsburgh, and you quickly realize her preferred style of cooking. Gallons of olive oil and huge tins of tomatoes line the pantry shelves. This is one of more than a dozen recipes Pam contributed to a benefit cookbook for her children's school. It's like a stew with Italian touches.

PREP: 20 minutes
COOK: 1 hour 10 minutes
MAKES: 4 servings

1	tablespoon vegetable oil
1	pound boneless beef chuck, cut into ½-inch cubes
1	medium-size onion, chopped
3	cups beef broth
½	can (28 ounces) crushed tomatoes (1¾ cups)
8	ounces fresh mushrooms, sliced
¾	teaspoon dried oregano
¾	teaspoon bottled chopped garlic
1	bay leaf
1	medium-size carrot, sliced
2	tablespoons cold water
4	teaspoons cornstarch
1	cup cooked rice
¼	cup dry red wine (optional)
	Fresh rosemary leaves or fresh basil leaves, for garnish (optional)

1. In large saucepan or kettle, heat oil over medium-high heat. Cook and stir half of the beef for 2 to 3 minutes or until brown. Remove with slotted spoon. Repeat with remaining beef and the onion. Return all beef and onion to pan. Stir in the beef broth, tomatoes, mushrooms, oregano, garlic and bay leaf. Bring to a boil. Reduce heat; simmer, covered, for 1 hour.

2. Uncover; add carrot. Return to a boil. Reduce heat; simmer, covered, for 7 minutes. Combine cold water and cornstarch; add to pan along with rice. Cook and stir until slightly thickened. Add wine, if desired; heat for 2 minutes. Discard bay leaf. If desired, garnish with rosemary or basil.

Per serving: 351 cal., 13 g total fat (4 g sat.), 82 mg chol., 914 mg sodium, 26 g carbo., 3 g fiber, 32 g pro.

Hearty Mushroom and Beef Soup

Chicken and Pasta Primavera

Chicken and Pasta Primavera

Steve Fetsko is learning from his kids to like vegetables. He and his wife, Angie, are parents to three children who will eat any green or orange food you put before them. It is Steve who struggles with anything beyond potatoes and corn. Angie likes this recipe because it freshens chicken and pasta with everyday vegetables like carrots and zucchini.

PREP: 15 minutes
COOK: about 10 minutes
MAKES: 6 servings

1	package (9 ounces) refrigerated spinach fettuccine or plain fettuccine
2	medium-size carrots, thinly sliced (1 cup)
1	medium-size zucchini, halved lengthwise and thinly sliced crosswise (1¼ cups)
¾	cup frozen whole kernel corn
¾	pound deli-roasted chicken, cut into ½-inch strips (about 2½ cups)
1½	cups chicken broth
4	teaspoons cornstarch
2	teaspoons finely shredded lemon peel
1	teaspoon dried basil
½	cup sour cream
2	tablespoons Dijon mustard
	Finely shredded Parmesan cheese

1. Cook pasta following package directions, adding carrots, zucchini and corn to water with pasta. Drain pasta and vegetables. Return all to saucepan; add chicken. (If the chicken has been refrigerated, place it in a colander. Pour the pasta, vegetables and cooking liquid over chicken to warm it; drain.)

2. In medium-size saucepan, combine broth, cornstarch, lemon peel and basil. Cook and stir over medium heat until thickened and bubbly. Cook and stir for 2 minutes more. Remove from heat. Stir in sour cream and mustard. Pour over pasta mixture; toss gently to coat.

3. Transfer pasta mixture to serving bowl. Sprinkle with cheese. Serve immediately.

Per serving: 334 cal., 10 g total fat (4 g sat.), 98 mg chol., 547 mg sodium, 34 g carbo., 3 g fiber, 27 g pro.

Shrimp Gravy

Shrimp Gravy

The pace on Edisto Island, 40 miles south of Charleston, South Carolina, is slow. Most menus are loaded with fresh seafood, including this low-country specialty of year-round resident Tom Kapp. It is often served at Trinity Episcopal Church after-service breakfasts. Kapp shared the recipe in a cookbook the congregation assembled to raise funds for the church.

PREP: 10 minutes
COOK: about 10 minutes
MAKES: 4 to 6 servings

5	strips bacon
8	scallions, trimmed and sliced (1 cup)
1	medium-size green pepper, seeded and chopped (¾ cup)
4	cloves garlic, finely chopped
1	tablespoon all-purpose flour
¼	teaspoon garlic salt
¼	teaspoon ground black pepper
¾	pound fresh mushrooms, sliced (4½ cups)
1½	pounds medium-size shrimp in shells, peeled and deveined
3	cups hot cooked grits

1. In large skillet, cook bacon until crisp. Remove bacon from skillet; drain on paper towels. Reserve 2 tablespoons drippings in skillet. Crumble bacon; set aside.

2. Heat reserved bacon drippings over medium heat. Add scallions, green pepper and garlic. Cook and stir until vegetables are tender. Stir in flour, garlic salt and black pepper. Stir in sliced mushrooms and shrimp. Cover; cook about 5 minutes or until shrimp turn pink and mushrooms are tender, stirring mixture occasionally.

3. To serve, immediately spoon mixture over hot cooked grits. Top each serving with crumbled bacon.

Per serving: 353 cal., 12 g total fat (4 g sat.), 209 mg chol., 887 mg sodium, 32 g carbo., 2 g fiber, 29 g pro.

Vegetable Lasagna

The hour before dinner can be nerve-frazzling with hungry children wailing for food. Jeni Wright of Des Moines developed this healthy vegetable lasagna for her two girls, Maya, 4, and Piper, 2. The girls nibble on extra cut veggies while the lasagna bakes. They still enjoy a piece when it comes out of the oven.

PREP: 30 minutes
BAKE: at 375° about 50 minutes
STAND: 10 minutes
MAKES: 6 servings

1	tablespoon olive oil
4	cups broccoli flowerets, chopped carrots, chopped zucchini and/or chopped yellow summer squash
1	cup light ricotta cheese or low-fat cottage cheese
3	tablespoons grated Parmesan cheese
¼	teaspoon black pepper
2	cups purchased pasta sauce, such as roasted tomato and garlic or roasted red pepper and onion
4	no-boil lasagna noodles
1	cup shredded part-skim mozzarella cheese (4 ounces)
½	cup cherry or grape tomatoes, quartered

1. Heat oven to 375°. In large nonstick skillet, heat oil over medium-high heat. Cook and stir vegetables in hot oil about 10 minutes or until vegetables are crisp-tender. Remove from heat.

2. In small bowl, combine ricotta cheese, Parmesan cheese and pepper.

3. To assemble, spoon about ½ cup of pasta sauce in bottom of 9×9×2-inch baking dish. Top with 2 lasagna noodles. Spread half of ricotta cheese mixture evenly over noodles. Top with half of vegetable mixture, half of remaining sauce, and half of mozzarella cheese. Repeat layering with remaining noodles, ricotta cheese mixture, vegetable mixture and sauce.

4. Cover with foil. Bake at 375° about 45 minutes or until mixture is heated through and noodles are tender. Uncover; sprinkle with tomatoes and remaining mozzarella cheese. Bake, uncovered, about 5 minutes or until cheese melts. Let stand for 10 minutes before serving.

Per serving: 236 cal., 9 g total fat (4 g sat. fat), 24 mg chol., 493 mg sodium, 25 g carbo., 4 g fiber, 13 g pro.

Vegetable Lasagna

Warm Fajita Salad

This recipe uses minimal oil to cook the meat and vegetables and salsa instead of salad dressing to keep it light and healthful.

PREP: 25 minutes
BAKE: tortilla strips at 400° for 8 to 10 minutes
COOK: about 10 minutes
MAKES: 4 servings

Tortilla Strips:
2	corn tortillas
⅛	teaspoon paprika
⅛	teaspoon chili powder

Beef-Vegetable Mixture:
¼	cup lime juice
¼	cup reduced-sodium chicken broth
1	tablespoon chopped fresh cilantro
2	cloves garlic, finely chopped
1½	teaspoons cornstarch
¾	pound boneless beef top sirloin steak, cut into thin, bite-size strips
½	teaspoon ground cumin
¼	teaspoon salt
¼	teaspoon black pepper
2	small onions, cut into thin wedges
2	small green and/or sweet red peppers, seeded and cut into thin strips
1	tablespoon vegetable oil

Salad:
1	package (10 ounces) torn mixed salad greens (8 cups)
12	cherry tomatoes, quartered
	Red or green salsa, for serving (optional)

1. Tortilla Strips: Heat oven to 400°. Cut corn tortillas into ⅛- to ¼-inch-wide strips. Place strips on a baking sheet. Coat with nonstick cooking spray. Combine paprika and chili powder; sprinkle over tortilla strips. Bake at 400° for 5 minutes. Toss and bake for 3 to 5 minutes more.

2. Beef-Vegetable Mixture: Combine lime juice, broth, cilantro, garlic and cornstarch. Set aside. Season beef with cumin, salt and black pepper; toss. Coat an unheated large skillet with nonstick cooking spray. Add onions and sweet peppers. Stir-fry over medium heat for 3 to 4 minutes or until vegetables are crisp-tender. Remove vegetables from skillet. Carefully add oil to skillet. Add beef strips; stir-fry 3 minutes or until done as desired. Push to side of skillet. Stir lime juice mixture; add to skillet. Cook and stir until thick and bubbly; cook and stir for 1 minute more. Return vegetables to pan; heat.

3. Salad: To assemble, arrange greens and tomatoes on four dinner plates. Divide beef-vegetable mixture among plates. Top with tortilla strips and serve with red or green salsa, if desired.

Per serving: 242 cal., 12 g total fat (4 g sat.), 57 mg chol., 235 mg sodium, 13 g carbo., 3 g fiber, 22 g pro.

Picadillo

Picadillo (pee-ka-DEE-yo) is a Latin American dish that has lots of variations—but almost all of them contain raisins for sweetness. Use it as a filling for stuffed peppers, make tacos with it or spoon it over hot cooked rice.

PREP: 25 minutes
COOK: 25 minutes
MAKES: 6 servings

1	pound lean ground beef
1	large onion, finely chopped (1 cup)
1	large green pepper, finely chopped (1 cup)
2	cloves garlic, finely chopped
1	can (8 ounces) tomato sauce
½	cup raisins
¼	cup dry sherry or chicken broth
¼	cup pimiento-stuffed green olives, sliced
1	tablespoon capers
½	teaspoon paprika
¼	teaspoon salt
6	medium-size green peppers and/or sweet red or yellow peppers or 3 cups hot cooked rice

1. In large skillet, cook beef, onion, chopped green pepper and garlic over medium heat until meat is brown and vegetables are tender. Drain off fat. Add tomato sauce, raisins, dry sherry, olives, capers, paprika and salt. Bring to a boil. Reduce heat; simmer, covered, for 15 minutes.

2. Meanwhile, if using, cut top third from whole sweet peppers (cutting either crosswise or lengthwise); discard seeds and membranes. Cook peppers, covered, in boiling water for 3 to 6 minutes or until crisp-tender. Remove from water and invert to drain. Fill peppers with cooked meat mixture or serve meat mixture over hot cooked rice.

Per serving in peppers: 270 cal., 13 g total fat (4 g sat.), 47 mg chol., 495 mg sodium, 21 g carbo., 3 g fiber, 15 g pro.

Skillet Pork Chops with Apples

Skillet Pork Chops with Apples

Certain kinds of apples are better for cooking than others because they keep their shape and don't turn mushy when exposed to heat. Good apple options for this skillet dish include Golden Delicious, Granny Smith, Jonathan or Rome Beauty.

PREP: 10 minutes
COOK: 13 to 15 minutes
MAKES: 4 servings

4	boneless pork loin chops, cut ¾ inch thick (about 1¼ pounds total)
	Salt and black pepper
2	tablespoons vegetable oil
2	medium-size onions, sliced and separated into rings (about 1 cup)
1	tablespoon chopped fresh marjoram leaves or 1 teaspoon dried marjoram
4	teaspoons coarse-grain brown mustard or Dijon mustard
2	red and/or green cooking apples, cored and cut into thin wedges

1. Season pork chops with salt and pepper. In large skillet, heat oil over medium-high heat. Brown chops in hot oil 4 minutes, turning once. Remove chops from skillet, reserving drippings in skillet.

2. Cook onion rings in reserved drippings over medium heat for 4 to 5 minutes or until crisp-tender, stirring occasionally. Reduce heat to medium-low. Sprinkle onions with about half of the marjoram. Place chops on onions. Spread chops with mustard. Arrange apples around chops; sprinkle all with remaining marjoram. Cover; cook for 5 to 6 minutes or until pork juices run clear. Serve apples, onions and pan juices with chops.

Per serving: 315 cal., 14 g total fat (3 g sat.), 77 mg chol., 162 mg sodium, 14 g carbo., 3 g fiber, 32 g pro.

Pork Roast with Baby Artichokes

PREP: 20 minutes
ROAST: at 375° for 1½ to 2 hours
STAND: 15 minutes
MAKES: 8 to 10 servings

¼	cup finely chopped fresh rosemary
¼	cup olive oil
6	cloves garlic, finely chopped
½	teaspoon salt
½	teaspoon black pepper
1½	pounds tiny new potatoes, halved
1	boneless top loin pork roast (double loin tied) (3 pounds)
6	to 8 baby artichokes
1	tablespoon lemon juice
2	cups packaged peeled baby carrots

1. Heat oven to 375°. In small bowl, combine rosemary, olive oil, garlic, salt and pepper. In large bowl, toss potatoes and half of the olive oil mixture. Place pork on rack in shallow roasting pan. Spread remaining olive oil mixture over pork. Arrange potato mixture around pork. Roast at 375°, stirring vegetables occasionally, for 1½ to 2 hours or until temperature registers 155° on an instant-read meat thermometer inserted in center of pork.

2. Meanwhile, wash artichokes; trim stems and remove loose outer leaves. Cut off ½ inch from top of each artichoke. Cut each artichoke into quarters lengthwise. Combine artichoke quarters and lemon juice; toss to mix. In covered large saucepan, cook artichokes and carrots in lightly salted boiling water for 10 minutes. Drain. Add artichokes and carrots to the roasting pan for the last 15 minutes of roasting, stirring to combine with potatoes. Remove pan from oven. Cover with foil; let stand for 15 minutes before serving.

Per serving: 385 cal., 15 g total fat (4 g sat.), 93 mg chol., 239 mg sodium, 20 g carbo., 4 g fiber, 40 g pro.

Balsamic Chicken and Vegetables

Serve this light and lovely entrée with quick-cooking brown rice.

PREP: 20 minutes
COOK: 9 to 11 minutes
MAKES: 4 servings

¼	cup bottled Italian salad dressing
2	tablespoons balsamic vinegar
1	tablespoon honey
⅛	to ¼ teaspoon red pepper flakes
2	tablespoons olive oil
1	pound chicken breast tenderloins
10	ounces fresh asparagus, ends trimmed, cut into 2-inch pieces, or 1 package (10 ounces) frozen cut asparagus, thawed and well drained
1	cup purchased shredded carrot or 2 medium-size carrots, shredded
1	small tomato, seeded and chopped

1. In small bowl, combine salad dressing, vinegar, honey and red pepper flakes.

2. In large skillet, heat oil over medium-high heat. Add chicken; cook for 5 to 6 minutes or until chicken is tender and no longer pink, turning once. Add half of the dressing mixture to skillet; turn chicken to coat. Transfer chicken to a serving platter; cover and keep warm.

3. Add asparagus and carrot to skillet. Cook and stir for 3 to 4 minutes or until asparagus is crisp-tender; transfer to serving platter.

4. Stir remaining dressing mixture; add to skillet. Cook and stir for 1 minute, scraping up browned bits from bottom of skillet. Drizzle dressing mixture over chicken and vegetables. Sprinkle with tomato.

Per serving: 269 cal., 12 g total fat (2 g sat.), 66 mg chol., 323 mg sodium, 12 g carbo., 2 g fiber, 27 g pro.

Creamy Chicken Enchiladas

If you don't have time to cook the chicken yourself, stop by the deli at your supermarket and buy two large or three small roasted chicken breasts. Minus the skin and bones, you should have about 1 pound of cooked chicken.

PREP: 40 minutes
BAKE: at 350° about 40 minutes
COOK: chicken about 15 minutes, spinach 3 to 5 minutes
STAND: 5 minutes
MAKES: 12 enchiladas

1	**pound boneless, skinless chicken breasts**
1	**package (10 ounces) frozen chopped spinach, thawed and squeezed dry**
4	**scallions, trimmed and thinly sliced (½ cup)**
2	**cups light sour cream**
½	**cup plain fat-free yogurt**
¼	**cup all-purpose flour**
½	**teaspoon ground cumin**
½	**teaspoon salt**
1	**cup milk**
2	**cans (4 ounces each) diced green chiles, drained**
12	**(7-inch) flour tortillas**
⅔	**cup shredded reduced-fat Cheddar or Monterey Jack cheese**
	Chopped tomato or salsa, for garnish (optional)
	Trimmed and thinly sliced scallions, for garnish (optional)

1. In large saucepan, combine chicken and enough water to cover. Bring to a boil. Reduce heat; cover; simmer for 12 to 14 minutes or until chicken is no longer pink. Remove chicken from saucepan. When cool enough to handle, use a fork to shred chicken into bite-size pieces. There should be about 3 cups.

2. Heat oven to 350°. In large bowl, combine chicken, spinach and sliced 4 scallions. For sauce, in medium-size bowl, combine sour cream, yogurt, flour, cumin and salt. Stir in milk and chiles.

3. For filling, combine half of the sauce and all of the chicken-spinach mixture. Divide filling among tortillas. Roll tortillas; place, seam sides down, in ungreased 13×9×2-inch baking dish. Spoon remaining sauce over tortillas.

4. Bake at 350° about 40 minutes or until heated through. Sprinkle with cheese; let stand for 5 minutes. To serve, if desired, transfer enchiladas to a serving platter and garnish with chopped tomato or salsa and additional scallions.

Per enchilada: 247 cal., 9 g total fat (4 g sat.), 44 mg chol., 395 mg sodium, 23 g carbo., 1 g fiber, 18 g pro.

Salmon with Feta Cheese and Pasta

Salmon with Feta Cheese and Pasta

Salmon has one of the highest concentrations of heart-healthy omega-3 fatty acids of any food out there. Make this dish with one of the whole-grain pastas that contain ground flaxseed and you will add more of that good stuff to your day.

PREP: 25 minutes
MAKES: 5 servings

½ **pound rotini pasta**
1 **teaspoon bottled chopped garlic**
¾ **pound skinless salmon fillet, cut into 1-inch pieces**
    Salt
4 **large plum tomatoes, chopped**
8 **scallions, trimmed and sliced (1 cup)**
⅓ **cup sliced pitted ripe olives**
3 **tablespoons chopped fresh basil leaves**
½ **teaspoon black pepper**
2 **teaspoons olive oil**
1 **package (4 ounces) crumbled feta cheese**

1. Cook pasta following package directions. Drain well. Return pasta to hot pan; cover to keep warm.

2. Lightly coat an unheated large nonstick skillet with nonstick cooking spray. Heat skillet over medium-high heat. Add garlic; cook and stir for 15 seconds. Lightly season fish pieces with salt. Add fish to skillet. Cook, turning occasionally, for 4 to 6 minutes or until fish flakes when tested with a fork. Stir in tomatoes, scallions, olives, basil and pepper. Heat through.

3. Add oil to drained pasta; toss to mix. Add salmon mixture and feta cheese; toss gently. To serve, transfer to a serving bowl.

Per serving: 373 cal., 13 g total fat (5 g sat.), 56 mg chol., 443 mg sodium, 41 g carbo., 3 g fiber, 24 g pro.

Ziti with Ricotta and Vegetables

Pictured on page 111.

PREP: 25 minutes
MAKES: 4 to 6 servings

½ **pound ziti or penne pasta**
2½ **cups broccoli flowerets**
1½ **cups fresh asparagus or green beans, trimmed and cut into 1-inch pieces**
2 **large ripe tomatoes, cored**
1 **cup light ricotta cheese**
¼ **cup chopped fresh basil leaves or 1 tablespoon dried basil**
4 **teaspoons chopped fresh thyme or 1 teaspoon dried thyme, crushed**
4 **teaspoons balsamic vinegar**
1 **tablespoon olive oil**
1 **clove garlic, finely chopped**
½ **teaspoon salt**
½ **teaspoon black pepper**
2 **tablespoons grated Parmesan or Romano cheese**

1. Cook pasta following package directions, omitting oil and salt and adding broccoli and asparagus or green beans for the last 3 minutes of cooking. Drain; return pasta and vegetables to pan.

2. Place a fine strainer over a bowl. Cut tomatoes in half; squeeze seeds and juice into strainer. With the back of a spoon, press seeds to extract juice; discard seeds, reserving tomatoes and juice.

3. Add ricotta cheese, basil, thyme, vinegar, oil, garlic, salt and pepper to tomato juice in bowl; mix well. Chop reserved tomatoes; stir into ricotta mixture. Add to hot cooked pasta and vegetables. Toss to combine. Serve immediately. Sprinkle each serving with Parmesan or Romano cheese.

Per serving: 366 cal., 8 g total fat (3 g sat.), 17 mg chol., 411 mg sodium, 57 g carbo., 5 g fiber, 17 g pro.

Chapter 7

Bring A Dish

Potluck Pleasers

Claim your reputation as a great cook
by taking these crowd-pleasing casseroles,
fresh salads and scrumptious side dishes
to your next potluck.

Pastitsio

Hawaiian Pineapple Baked Beans

Virginia Ogan's uncle once ribbed her mother about the baked beans she took to the family reunion. "He joked that my mom added pineapple," Virginia, of Osceola, Iowa, says. The next year, Virginia and her sisters brought the beans. As a practical joke, they added pineapple. "My uncle was speechless!" Virginia says. The recipe, it turns out, is a keeper.

PREP: 15 minutes
BAKE: at 350° about 1 hour
MAKES: 8 to 10 side-dish servings

- 1 **pound ground beef**
- 1 **medium-size onion, chopped (½ cup)**
- ½ **cup ketchup**
- ½ **cup bottled hot-style barbecue sauce**
- 2 **tablespoons packed light-brown sugar**
- 1 **can (15 to 16 ounces) pork and beans in tomato sauce**
- 1 **can (15 ounces) chili beans with chili gravy**
- 1 **can (8 ounces) pineapple tidbits (juice pack), drained**

1. Heat oven to 350°. In large skillet, cook ground beef and onion over medium-high heat until meat is brown and onion is tender. Drain off fat. Stir in ketchup, barbecue sauce and brown sugar. Stir in pork and beans, chili beans and pineapple.

2. Transfer bean mixture to 2-quart casserole. Bake at 350° about 1 hour or until heated through.

Per serving: 322 cal., 14 g total fat (5 g sat.), 41 mg chol., 833 mg sodium, 35 g carbo., 6 g fiber, 15 g pro.

Hawaiian Pineapple Baked Beans

Yum-Yum Ribbon Salad

Yum-Yum Ribbon Salad

Quilter Jane Quinn of Bozeman, Montana, tinkers with recipes the same way she plays with quilt blocks. At an annual quilt show, Jane and several of her quilting colleagues accepted the challenge to design a quilt block that represents a favorite salad recipe. Jane used one of her eye-catching red, white and green quilt blocks as inspiration for this colorful gelatin salad.

PREP: 25 minutes
CHILL: 7 hours total
MAKES: 15 side-dish servings

1	package (6 ounces) strawberry- or raspberry-flavored gelatin
1	package (3 ounces) lemon-flavored gelatin
1	cup boiling water
1	cup miniature marshmallows
1	package (3 ounces) cream cheese, softened
¾	cup mayonnaise
1	can (8 ounces) crushed pineapple, undrained
½	cup heavy cream
1	package (3 ounces) lime-flavored gelatin
	Whipped cream, for serving (optional)

1. Prepare strawberry gelatin following package directions. Pour into 13×9×2-inch baking dish. Chill about 1 hour or until almost firm (sticky to touch).

2. In large bowl, dissolve lemon-flavored gelatin in the 1 cup boiling water. Add marshmallows; whisk until marshmallows melt. Whisk in cream cheese and mayonnaise until combined. Stir in pineapple. In small bowl, beat cream until soft peaks form. Gently fold whipped cream into pineapple mixture. Carefully spoon over chilled gelatin, distributing pineapple evenly. Refrigerate about 1 hour or until almost firm (sticky to touch).

3. Prepare lime-flavored gelatin following package directions. Refrigerate about 45 minutes or until partially set (the consistency of unbeaten egg whites). Pour over chilled pineapple mixture. Cover and refrigerate 4 hours or until firm.

4. To serve, cut salad into squares. If desired, top with a spoonful of whipped cream.

Per serving: 238 cal., 14 g total fat (4 g sat.), 23 mg chol., 145 mg sodium, 27 g carbo., 0 g fiber, 3 g pro.

Truck Stop Potatoes

Some truck-stop food is so good it makes you want to hit the road just so you can stop to eat. Decatur, Alabama, caterer John Harris adapted a recipe served at an Idaho truck stop for these locally famous potatoes. It appeared in a cookbook benefiting Decatur General Hospital. Your doctor might not approve, but your friends certainly will.

PREP: 30 minutes
BAKE: at 350° about 30 minutes
STAND: 10 minutes
MAKES: 10 side-dish servings

2	to 2¼ pounds small red potatoes, coarsely chopped (about 6 cups)
1	large onion, chopped (¾ cup)
1	cup sour cream
1	cup shredded Monterey Jack cheese (4 ounces)
1	cup shredded sharp Cheddar cheese (4 ounces)
½	teaspoon salt
¼	to ½ teaspoon cayenne pepper
1	can (14½ ounces) diced tomatoes, drained
½	cup sour cream, for serving (optional)
	Chopped fresh tomato, chopped avocado and sliced scallion, for serving (optional)

1. Heat oven to 350°. In large covered saucepan, cook potatoes and onion in large amount of boiling water about 20 minutes or until tender. Drain; return to saucepan. Stir in the 1 cup sour cream, the Monterey Jack cheese, Cheddar cheese, salt and cayenne pepper. Stir in canned tomatoes. Spoon into 11×7×1½-inch baking dish.

2. Bake at 350° about 30 minutes or until heated through. Cover; let stand for 10 minutes before serving. If desired, top with additional ½ cup sour cream (in mounds), fresh tomato, avocado and scallions.

Per serving: 220 cal., 12 g total fat (8 g sat.), 32 mg chol., 333 mg sodium, 20 g carbo., 2 g fiber, 9 g pro.

Truck Stop Potatoes

MaMa's Dinner Rolls

MaMa's Dinner Rolls

Ronnie Hawkins' grandmother, MaMa, learned to cook growing up in Texas and Louisiana. Later, as the wife of the bishop of the Church of the Living God on Chicago's south side, she had lots of opportunities to share her Southern cooking with others. Now Ronnie, a caterer in Des Moines, makes these airy dinner rolls for her family, her customers and her own pastor.

PREP: 40 minutes
RISE: 1¾ to 2¼ hours
BAKE: at 350° about 20 minutes
MAKES: about 30 rolls

¼	cup warm water (105° to 115°)
2	packages active dry yeast
1	cup milk
1	cup butter
1	cup sugar
½	teaspoon salt
3	eggs
6	to 6½ cups all-purpose flour
2	tablespoons butter, melted

1. In small bowl or glass measure, combine warm water and yeast. Stir to mix well.

2. In saucepan, heat and stir milk, the 1 cup butter, sugar and salt just until mixture is warm (120° to 130°) and butter has almost melted. In very large bowl, combine milk mixture, yeast mixture and eggs. Stir in 4½ cups of the flour. Cover and let rise in a warm place until nearly double (1 to 1½ hours). Stir dough down. Using wooden spoon, stir in as much of the remaining flour as possible.

3. Turn dough out onto floured surface. Knead in enough of any remaining flour to make a moderately soft dough that is smooth and elastic (3 to 5 minutes total). Cover; let rest 10 minutes. (Dough will be soft.)

4. Brush three 9×1½-inch round baking pans with some of the melted butter; set aside. On lightly floured surface, roll dough to ½-inch thickness. Using 2½-inch round cutter, cut dough into about 30 rounds, rerolling dough as necessary. Brush rounds with remaining melted butter.

5. Fold each dough round nearly in half, buttered side inside, so that top slightly overlaps bottom. Divide rolls evenly among prepared pans. Cover; let rise in warm place until almost double (about 45 minutes).

6. Heat oven to 350°. Bake at 350° about 20 minutes or until golden. Invert onto wire racks to cool slightly; serve warm.

Per roll: 182 cal., 8 g total fat (5 g sat.), 40 mg chol., 116 mg sodium, 25 g carbo., 1 g fiber, 4 g pro.

Grandma's Spaghetti Casserole

Serve this cheesy baked pasta dish with a simple green salad and garlic bread.

PREP: 30 minutes
BAKE: at 350° about 40 minutes
STAND: 5 to 10 minutes
MAKES: 4 to 6 main-dish servings

½	**pound spaghetti**
½	**pound ground beef**
1	**medium-size onion, chopped**
½	**cup chopped green pepper**
1	**can (14½ ounces) diced tomatoes, undrained**
1	**can (10¾ ounces) condensed tomato soup**
½	**teaspoon black pepper**
1	**package (8 ounces) shredded Cheddar cheese (2 cups)**
4	**strips bacon, crisp-cooked, drained and crumbled**

1. Heat oven to 350°. Grease 2-quart casserole. Cook spaghetti following package directions. Drain. Set aside prepared casserole and spaghetti.

2. In large skillet, cook and stir ground beef, onion and green pepper over medium-high heat until beef is brown. Drain off fat. Stir in tomatoes, soup and black pepper. Bring just to a boil. Add 1 cup of the cheese, stirring until melted.

3. Add spaghetti and bacon to tomato mixture, tossing to combine. Transfer mixture to prepared casserole.

4. Bake, covered, at 350° about 40 minutes or until bubbly and heated through. Uncover; sprinkle with remaining cheese. Let stand for 5 to 10 minutes or until cheese melts.

Per serving: 675 cal., 31 g total fat (16 g sat.), 100 mg chol., 1,007 mg sodium, 61 g carbo., 3 g fiber, 35 g pro.

Summer Asparagus

Trim the woody lower part of the stem from fresh asparagus by starting at the base of each spear and bending the spear several times—working toward the tip—until you hit a spot where it breaks easily.

PREP: 10 minutes
COOK: 6 minutes
MAKES: 8 side-dish servings

1	tablespoon balsamic vinegar
1	tablespoon red-wine vinegar
2	teaspoons Dijon mustard
⅛	teaspoon salt
⅛	teaspoon black pepper
½	cup olive oil
1	tablespoon chopped fresh chervil leaves
1	teaspoon finely chopped shallot
2	pounds fresh asparagus, trimmed (stem ends peeled, if thick)
¾	pound grape tomatoes, halved
3	ounces feta cheese, crumbled

1. In small bowl, whisk balsamic and red-wine vinegars, mustard, salt and pepper. Slowly whisk in oil in thin stream. Stir in chervil and shallot. Cover; set aside until ready to use.

2. Steam asparagus about 6 minutes or until tender.

3. On large platter, arrange asparagus and tomatoes. Sprinkle with feta cheese. Drizzle with half of dressing. Serve remaining dressing on the side.

Per serving: 174 cal., 16 g total fat (3 g sat.), 9 mg chol., 190 mg sodium, 5 g carbo., 2 g fiber, 4 g pro.

German-Style Pasta Salad

Smoked salmon, dill and capers are a classic combination. Here they add flavor and flair to a simple macaroni salad.

PREP: 40 minutes
CHILL: 4 to 24 hours
MAKES: 10 to 12 side-dish servings

¾	pound medium shell macaroni
2	hard-cooked eggs, chopped
1	package (4 ounces) thinly sliced smoked salmon (lox-style), chopped
⅓	cup chopped red onion
2	tablespoons capers, drained
1	cup sour cream
⅓	cup milk
¼	cup chopped fresh dill
2	tablespoons mayonnaise
½	teaspoon salt
¼	teaspoon black pepper
	Milk

1. Cook pasta following package directions; drain. Rinse with cold water; drain again.

2. In large bowl, combine cooked pasta, eggs, salmon, onion and capers. In small bowl, combine sour cream, the ⅓ cup milk, dill, mayonnaise, salt and pepper.

3. Pour sour cream mixture over pasta mixture. Toss lightly to coat. Cover and refrigerate for 4 to 24 hours. Before serving, if necessary, stir in additional milk to moisten.

Per serving: 230 cal., 9 g total fat (4 g sat.), 58 mg chol., 441 mg sodium, 27 g carbo., 1 g fiber, 9 g pro.

Macaroni and Cheese Casserole

Diced ham adds smoky flavor to this homey comfort-food favorite.

PREP: 5 minutes
BAKE: at 350° for 30 to 40 minutes
STAND: 10 minutes
MAKES: 8 main-dish servings

4	eggs, lightly beaten
1½	cups milk
2	tablespoons chopped fresh parsley leaves
½	teaspoon salt
¼	teaspoon black pepper
¾	pound hot cooked macaroni
1	package (8 ounces) shredded Cheddar cheese (2 cups)
½	pound diced ham (optional)
3	tablespoons bread crumbs
2	tablespoons grated Parmesan cheese
2	tablespoons unsalted butter, cut into pieces

1. Heat oven to 350°. Coat 12×7×1½-inch baking dish with nonstick cooking spray. In large bowl, combine eggs, milk, parsley, salt and pepper. Add macaroni, cheese and diced ham, if using, to milk mixture. Stir to mix well.

2. Transfer macaroni mixture to prepared baking dish. Sprinkle top with even layer of bread crumbs. Sprinkle with Parmesan cheese. Dot with butter.

3. Bake at 350° for 30 to 40 minutes or until bubbly and hot. Let stand for 10 minutes before serving.

Per serving: 281 cal., 17 g total fat (9 g sat.), 148 mg chol., 414 mg sodium, 18 g carbo., 1 g fiber, 15 g pro.

Crunchy Chicken Fingers

Kids will go crazy for these restaurant-style chicken fingers. They're dipped in seasoned sour cream and then in crushed herbed stuffing mix to give them loads of flavor in every juicy bite. Yum!

PREP: 20 minutes
BAKE: at 375° about 25 minutes
MAKES: 10 to 12 main-dish servings

8	medium boneless, skinless chicken breast halves
1	cup sour cream
2	tablespoons lemon juice
1	tablespoon Worcestershire sauce
1	teaspoon paprika
¼	teaspoon celery salt
¼	teaspoon black pepper
1	package (8 ounces) herb-seasoned stuffing mix, coarsely crushed
4	tablespoons (½ stick) butter or margarine, melted

1. Heat oven to 375°. Cut chicken into ¾-inch-wide strips. In shallow bowl, combine sour cream, lemon juice, Worcestershire sauce, paprika, celery salt and pepper. In another shallow bowl, place crushed stuffing mix.

2. Dip chicken strips into sour cream mixture; coat with crushed stuffing mix. In two large shallow baking pans, arrange chicken strips. Pieces shouldn't touch. Drizzle melted butter over chicken.

3. Bake at 375° about 25 minutes or until chicken is no longer pink, rotating pans after 15 minutes.

Per serving: 312 cal., 12 g total fat (6 g sat.), 89 mg chol., 496 mg sodium, 19 g carbo., 2 g fiber, 30 g pro.

Crunchy Chicken Fingers

Spicy Penne Pasta Toss

PREP: 20 minutes
COOK: about 30 minutes
MAKES: 8 to 10 servings

2	tablespoons olive oil
1	pound boneless, skinless chicken breasts, cut into 1-inch chunks
3	hot Italian sausages, cut into coins
4	cloves garlic, chopped
1	can (28 ounces) whole peeled tomatoes, chopped
1	can (15 ounces) tomato sauce
1	can (6 ounces) tomato paste
1	teaspoon dried basil
½	teaspoon dried oregano
1	sweet red pepper, cored, seeded and cut into ¾-inch pieces
½	pound medium-size shrimp, shelled and deveined
1	pound penne pasta
½	cup grated pecorino Romano cheese

1. In large saucepan, heat oil over medium-high heat. Add chicken and sausage; cook for 5 minutes, stirring occasionally. Add garlic and cook for 1 minute. Stir in undrained tomatoes, tomato sauce, tomato paste, basil, oregano, ½ teaspoon salt and ¼ teaspoon black pepper. Bring to a boil. Reduce heat; simmer for 10 minutes, stirring occasionally. Add sweet pepper and simmer 10 minutes. Stir in shrimp; cook about 3 minutes or until shrimp are pink and firm.

2. When the sauce is halfway done, prepare pasta following package directions. Drain, reserving ½ cup of pasta water.

3. Stir pasta and cheese into sauce; cook for 1 minute. Add some pasta water if sauce is too thick.

Per serving: 531 cal., 18 g total fat (6 g sat.), 109 mg chol., 1,151 mg sodium, 55 g carbo., 5 g fiber, 36 g pro.

Sweet Chili

Cincinnatians like their chili served over spaghetti. This well-spiced version—with brown sugar to heighten the flavors—is served over elbow macaroni.

PREP: 10 minutes
COOK: about 45 to 50 minutes
STAND: 10 minutes
MAKES: 8 main-dish servings

2	pounds ground beef
2	large onions, chopped (1½ cups)
2	cloves garlic, finely chopped
2	teaspoons chili powder
2	teaspoons salt
1	teaspoon ground cumin
1	teaspoon black pepper
1	teaspoon dried oregano
1	can (28 ounces) whole tomatoes
1	can (28 ounces) tomato sauce
1	can (16 ounces) red kidney beans, drained and rinsed
½	cup packed light-brown sugar
1	pound elbow macaroni

1. In large nonstick pot, cook beef, onions and garlic until beef is brown, stirring occasionally. Add chili powder, salt, cumin, pepper and oregano. Cook about 2 minutes more or until fragrant.

2. Drain liquid from tomatoes into pot; roughly chop tomatoes and add to pot. Fill tomato can with water and add to pot along with tomato sauce, beans and brown sugar. Bring to a boil. Reduce heat; simmer, uncovered, for 30 to 35 minutes. Let stand for 10 minutes before serving.

3. Cook pasta following package directions. Drain. Serve chili over cooked pasta.

Per serving: 704 cal., 30 g total fat (11 g sat.), 85 mg chol., 1,530 mg sodium, 78 g carbo., 9 g fiber, 31 g pro.

Hot Chicken Salad

Here's a creamy and satisfying twist on traditional chicken salad that will take the chill off even the coldest nights. Serve it with steamed green beans and crusty whole grain bread or rolls.

PREP: 30 minutes
BAKE: at 400° for 30 to 35 minutes
STAND: 10 minutes
MAKES: 12 main-dish servings

1	cup coarsely crushed potato chips
⅔	cup finely chopped almonds
6	cups cubed cooked chicken*
6	ribs celery, chopped (3 cups)
1	can (10¾ ounces) condensed cream of chicken soup
1	package (8 ounces) shredded mozzarella cheese (2 cups)
2	cups sour cream or plain yogurt
¼	cup chopped onion
1	teaspoon dried thyme or basil
4	hard-cooked eggs, chopped

1. Heat oven to 400°. In small bowl, combine potato chips and almonds. In very large bowl, combine chicken, celery, soup, cheese, sour cream, onion and thyme. Gently fold in eggs.

2. Transfer chicken mixture to 13×9×2-inch baking dish. Sprinkle with potato chip mixture. Bake at 400° for 30 to 35 minutes or until heated through. Let stand for 10 minutes before serving.

*Note: About 2¼ pounds boneless chicken breasts will yield 6 cups chopped cooked chicken.

Per serving: 398 cal., 25 g total fat (10 g sat.), 168 mg chol., 437 mg sodium, 9 g carbo., 2 g fiber, 33 g pro.

Carnita Enchiladas

PREP: 15 minutes
BAKE: at 375° about 25 minutes
COOK: 10 to 12 minutes
MAKES: 8 main-dish servings

1	tablespoon vegetable oil
1	pound lean ground beef
2	medium-size onions, chopped (1 cup)
1	medium-size potato (about 8 ounces), peeled and chopped
1	medium-size tomato, chopped
1	can (15 ounces) black beans, drained and rinsed
1	teaspoon chili powder
½	teaspoon garlic powder
2	cans (10 ounces each) enchilada sauce
16	(6- or 7-inch) corn tortillas
1½	cups shredded Cheddar cheese

1. Heat oven to 375°. Coat 13×9×2-inch baking dish with nonstick cooking spray.

2. In large nonstick skillet, heat oil over medium-high heat. Add ground beef and onions. Cook about 5 minutes or until light brown. Add potato and tomato. Cook, covered, for 5 to 7 minutes or until potato softens. Add beans, chili powder, 1 teaspoon salt and garlic powder to mixture in skillet. Mix until well combined. Remove from heat.

3. Spread ¼ cup of the enchilada sauce on bottom of baking dish. Tear up 8 of the tortillas and evenly distribute over sauce. Evenly cover with meat and bean mixture. Pour ½ cup enchilada sauce evenly over meat layer. Tear up remaining 8 tortillas and evenly distribute over sauce. Pour remaining sauce over top and sprinkle with cheese.

4. Bake at 375° about 25 minutes or until mixture is bubbly and cheese has melted.

Per serving: 457 cal., 26 g total fat (10 g sat.), 65 mg chol., 1,157 mg sodium, 39 g carbo., 7 g fiber, 21 g pro.

Layered Southwest Bean Salad

PREP: 30 minutes
CHILL: 4 to 24 hours
MAKES: 8 to 12 servings

Layered Salad:

4	cups shredded iceberg lettuce
2	cans (15 ounces each) black beans, rinsed and drained
2	medium-size red onions, chopped (1 cup)
1	can (4 ounces) chopped green chiles, drained
2	large green peppers and/or sweet red peppers, seeded and chopped (2 cups)
2	tablespoons chopped fresh cilantro leaves

Creamy Lime Dressing:

1½	cups sour cream
2	tablespoons lime juice
1	teaspoon chili powder
½	teaspoon salt
¼	teaspoon garlic powder
1	large tomato, seeded and chopped (¾ cup)

1. Layered Salad: In deep 3-quart bowl, place lettuce. Layer on beans, onions, chiles, green peppers and cilantro.

2. Creamy Lime Dressing: In small bowl, combine sour cream, lime juice, chili powder, salt and garlic powder. Spread dressing over top of salad, sealing it to edge of bowl. Cover; refrigerate for 4 to 24 hours.

3. To serve, gently toss salad to coat vegetables with dressing; sprinkle with tomato.

Per serving: 173 cal., 8 g total fat (5 g sat.), 16 mg chol., 492 mg sodium, 22 g carbo., 7 g fiber, 9 g pro.

Layered Southwest Bean Salad

Pastitsio

Pictured on page 129.

PREP: 45 minutes
BAKE: at 350° about 35 minutes
STAND: 15 minutes
MAKES: 8 main-dish servings

Meat Sauce:
1	pound lean ground beef
1	large onion, chopped (¾ cup)
1	can (8 ounces) tomato sauce
¼	cup dry red wine
1	stick cinnamon (4 inches long)

Pasta Mixture:
½	pound penne pasta
¾	cup milk
2	eggs, lightly beaten
2	tablespoons butter, melted

Cream Sauce:
2	tablespoons butter
2	tablespoons all-purpose flour
¼	teaspoon salt
⅛	teaspoon pepper
1½	cups milk
3	eggs, lightly beaten
1	cup shredded kasseri* or Romano cheese (4 ounces)

1. Meat Sauce: Heat oven to 350°. Grease 13×9×2-inch baking dish. In large skillet, cook ground beef and onion until meat is brown and onion is tender. Drain off fat. Stir in tomato sauce, wine and cinnamon. Bring to a boil. Reduce heat; simmer, covered, for 30 minutes, stirring occasionally. Discard cinnamon stick. Set aside.

2. Pasta Mixture: Cook pasta following package directions. Drain. Rinse and drain again. In large bowl, toss pasta with the ¾ cup milk, 2 eggs and 2 tablespoons melted butter. Set mixture aside.

3. Cream Sauce: In small saucepan, melt 2 tablespoons butter over medium heat. Stir in flour, salt and pepper until smooth. Gradually add the 1½ cups milk. Cook and stir until mixture is thick and bubbly. Gradually stir hot mixture into the 3 eggs.

4. Layer half of pasta mixture in prepared dish. Spread with meat mixture. Sprinkle with ⅓ cup of cheese. Top with remaining pasta; sprinkle with another ⅓ cup of cheese. Pour cream sauce over all; sprinkle with remaining cheese.

5. Bake, covered, at 350° for 20 minutes. Uncover and bake about 15 minutes or until knife inserted in center comes out clean. Let stand for 15 minutes before serving.

*Note: Kasseri cheese is a hard cheese widely used in Greek cooking. It has a sharp flavor that is quite similar to Romano cheese, which is more readily available in supermarkets. Parmesan cheese also would work.

Per serving: 553 cal., 30 g total fat (12 g sat. fat), 241 mg chol., 657 mg sodium, 31 g carbo., 2 g fiber, 36 g pro.

Lasagna Blanca

This elegant take on traditional lasagna is called "blanca" because the cheesy sauce for these spiraled lasagna rolls is creamy-white, not red.

PREP: 1 hour
BAKE: at 350° about 35 minutes
STAND: 10 minutes
MAKES: 12 main-dish servings

12	lasagna noodles
1	pound spicy bulk pork sausage
4	scallions, trimmed and chopped (½ cup)
½	cup chopped fresh mushrooms
1	cup cottage cheese
½	package (8 ounces) cream cheese
1½	cups shredded Monterey Jack or Cheddar cheese (6 ounces)
½	teaspoon garlic powder
⅛	teaspoon black pepper
1	tablespoon butter
1	tablespoon all-purpose flour
⅛	teaspoon dried tarragon
⅛	teaspoon black pepper
1	cup milk

1. Heat oven to 350°. Grease 13×9×2-inch baking dish. Cook lasagna noodles following package directions. Drain. Rinse with cold water; drain again.

2. In large skillet, cook sausage, scallions and mushrooms until sausage is brown and vegetables are tender, breaking sausage into small pieces. Drain off fat. Set aside.

3. In medium-size bowl, combine cottage cheese, cream cheese, ½ cup of the Monterey Jack cheese, garlic powder and ⅛ teaspoon pepper.

4. Place noodles on clean surface. Spread cheese filling evenly over noodles. Sprinkle sausage mixture on top. Roll each noodle into spiral. Place lasagna rolls, seam sides down, in prepared baking dish.

5. For sauce, in small saucepan, melt butter. Stir in flour, tarragon and ⅛ teaspoon pepper. Add milk. Cook and stir until slightly thick and bubbly. Remove from heat. Stir in ½ cup of the Monterey Jack cheese. Pour sauce over pasta spirals.

6. Bake, covered, at 350° for 25 minutes. Remove cover; sprinkle with remaining Monterey Jack cheese. Bake about 10 minutes or until heated through. Let stand 10 minutes before serving.

Per serving: 317 cal., 17 g total fat (9 g sat.), 54 mg chol., 378 mg sodium, 21 g carbo., 1 g fiber, 16 g pro.

Chinese Cabbage Slaw

Chinese cabbage (also called napa cabbage) has long, pale yellow-green leaves in a tightly packed head. It has a mild, faintly sweet flavor.

PREP: 25 minutes
CHILL: 4 to 24 hours
MAKES: 8 side-dish servings

1	**medium-size cucumber, halved lengthwise and thinly sliced crosswise**
1	**cup fresh pea pods, halved**
¼	**cup rice vinegar**
1	**tablespoon vegetable oil**
2	**teaspoons dark Asian sesame oil**
½	**teaspoon sugar**
¼	**teaspoon salt**
¼	**teaspoon red pepper flakes**
4	**cups shredded Chinese cabbage**
½	**cup coarsely chopped honey-roasted peanuts or dry roasted peanuts**

1. In large bowl, combine cucumber and pea pods. In small bowl, whisk together vinegar, vegetable oil, sesame oil, sugar, salt and red pepper flakes. Pour mixture over cucumber and pea pods, stirring to coat. Cover and refrigerate for 4 to 24 hours.

2. Up to 2 hours before serving, stir cabbage into cucumber mixture. Cover and refrigerate until ready to serve. Just before serving, sprinkle salad with nuts.

Per serving: 86 cal., 7 g total fat (1 g sat.), 0 mg chol., 108 mg sodium, 6 g carbo., 2 g fiber, 3 g pro.

Nutty Wild Rice Salad

To save on last-minute prep time of this hearty salad, you can cook, cool and refrigerate the wild rice up to a day ahead of serving.

PREP: 20 minutes
COOK: about 45 minutes
STAND: 1 hour
MAKES: 8 to 10 servings

1	**can (14 ounces) chicken broth**
1	**cup wild rice, rinsed and drained**
¾	**cup shredded carrot***
¾	**cup chopped pecans, toasted**
½	**cup dried currants**
2	**scallions, trimmed and sliced (¼ cup)**
3	**tablespoons vegetable oil**
2	**tablespoons balsamic vinegar**
½	**teaspoon curry powder**
½	**teaspoon dry mustard**
¼	**teaspoon garlic powder**
	Salt
	Black pepper

1. In medium-size saucepan, combine chicken broth and uncooked wild rice. Bring to a boil; reduce heat. Simmer, covered, about 45 minutes or until wild rice is tender and most of liquid is absorbed. Let stand at room temperature for 1 hour.

2. Stir carrot, pecans, currants and scallions into wild rice mixture. In screw-top jar, combine oil, balsamic vinegar, curry powder, dry mustard and garlic powder. Cover and shake well. Pour over wild rice mixture; toss to coat. Season to taste with salt and pepper.

***Note:** If you like, use purchased shredded carrots to save preparation time.

Per serving: 225 cal., 13 g total fat (1 g sat.), 1 mg chol., 293 mg sodium, 25 g carbo., 3 g fiber, 5 g pro.

Cucumber-Orzo Salad

Honey adds a little sweetness and white balsamic vinegar a hint of sharpness to the vinaigrette for this light and refreshing pasta salad.

PREP: 25 minutes
CHILL: 4 to 24 hours
MAKES: 8 side-dish servings

1	cup orzo (rosamarina) pasta
1	small cucumber, seeded and chopped
½	cup chopped sweet red pepper
¼	cup finely chopped red onion
¼	cup olive oil
¼	cup white-balsamic vinegar
1	tablespoon honey
1	teaspoon finely shredded lemon peel
½	teaspoon salt
¼	teaspoon black pepper
¼	cup chopped fresh flat-leaf parsley

1. Cook orzo following package directions. Drain. Rinse with cold water; drain again.

2. In large bowl, combine orzo, cucumber, sweet red pepper and red onion. In small bowl, whisk together olive oil, vinegar, honey, lemon peel, salt and black pepper; add to orzo mixture. Stir gently to combine. Cover and refrigerate for 4 to 24 hours.

3. Just before serving, stir in parsley.

Per serving: 165 cal., 7 g total fat (1 g sat. fat), 0 mg chol., 150 mg sodium, 22 g carbo., 1 g fiber, 3 g pro.

Chapter 8

Let's Do Lunch

Hand-Held Favorites

Whether you want just a quick bite or a hand-held meal for movie or game night, these no-utensils-needed recipes make for effortless, casual eating.

Roast Beef and Pepper Sandwiches

The Picasso

The clientele of Palmer's Deli & Market in Urbandale, Iowa, is loyal—and for good reason. One customer orders the same sandwich every day and it is ready for her before she walks in the door. The name of this "work of art" refers to the meticulous layering of focaccia with meat, cheese and tomatoes. It is a favorite at Palmer's.

PREP: 20 minutes
MAKES: 6 wedges

1	**Italian flat bread (focaccia) (12 ounces)**
¼	**cup bottled creamy garlic salad dressing**
½	**pound thinly sliced hard salami**
4	**plum tomatoes, thinly sliced**
½	**pound thinly sliced provolone cheese**
1	**jar (7 ounces) roasted sweet red peppers, drained**
½	**pound thinly sliced cooked ham**
4	**leaves romaine lettuce**

1. Using serrated knife, slice bread in half horizontally. On hot griddle, in large skillet or under broiler, toast cut sides of bread.

2. Spread dressing on cut sides of loaf. Arrange salami, tomatoes, provolone cheese, sweet peppers, ham and romaine leaves over dressing. Cover with remaining half loaf, cut side down. Cut sandwich into wedges.

Per wedge: 557 cal., 33 g total fat (14 g sat.) 77 mg chol., 1,647 mg sodium, 35 g carbo., 3 g fiber, 31 g pro.

The Picasso

Extra-Saucy Chicken Sandwiches

Extra-Saucy Chicken Sandwiches

Recipes with yields that easily increase or decrease depending on the number of people at the dinner table are filed in a special spot in Diana Meinders' recipe box. Sometimes it is just the Des Moines grandmother and her husband, Kevin, for dinner. Other times their adult children and a grandchild drop by and stay for a meal. This tasty recipe for two easily doubles or triples.

PREP: 20 minutes
COOK: 8 to 10 minutes
MAKES: 3 sandwiches

1	tablespoon vegetable oil
1	small onion, halved crosswise and thinly sliced
1	pound skinless, boneless chicken breast halves, cut into bite-size strips
½	jar (14 to 16 ounces) Cheddar cheese pasta sauce (about ¾ cup)
1	tablespoon Worcestershire sauce
6	slices marbled rye bread, toasted
1	small tomato, sliced
6	strips bacon, crisp-cooked and drained (optional)

1. In large skillet, heat oil over medium-high heat. Add onion and chicken. Cook and stir for 4 to 5 minutes or until chicken is no longer pink. Add pasta sauce and Worcestershire sauce. Heat through.

2. To serve, spoon chicken and sauce mixture over half of the bread slices. Top with tomato and, if desired, bacon. Top with remaining bread slices.

Per sandwich: 491 cal., 18 g total fat (5 g sat.), 114 mg chol., 1,084 mg sodium, 38 g carbo., 4 g fiber, 43 g pro.

Taco Pizza

Taco Pizza

What do you do when you need lunch on the table fast for your hungry spouse and children? Jill Moberly of Des Moines lets 4-year-old Jacob press the dough into the pan and sprinkle on the toppers. This quick recipe adapts to the tastes of both adults and kids, depending on the optional garnishes used.

PREP: 15 minutes
BAKE: at 400° about 20 minutes
MAKES: 6 slices

- ½ **pound lean ground beef and/or bulk pork sausage**
- 1 **medium-size green pepper, seeded and chopped (¾ cup)**
- 1 **tube (11½ ounces) refrigerated corn bread twists**
- ½ **cup purchased salsa**
- 3 **cups shredded taco-blend cheese (12 ounces)**
  Crushed tortilla chips, for serving (optional)
  Sour cream, for serving (optional)
  Chopped tomato, for serving (optional)
  Chopped scallions, for serving (optional)

1. Heat oven to 400°. Grease 12-inch pizza pan. In large skillet, cook beef and green pepper over medium heat until beef is brown. Drain off fat.

2. Unroll corn bread dough (do not separate into strips). Press dough onto bottom and up edges of prepared pizza pan. Spread salsa on top of dough. Sprinkle with meat mixture and cheese.

3. Bake at 400° about 20 minutes or until bottom of crust is golden brown (to check, lift slightly with spatula). If desired, top with crushed tortilla chips, sour cream, tomato and/or scallions. Cut into wedges to serve.

Per slice: 451 cal., 30 g total fat (15 g sat.), 73 mg chol., 901 mg sodium, 26 g carbo., 1 g fiber, 22 g pro.

Zippy Zucchini Pizza

Gardener and dietitian Linda Jacobsen talks the talk and walks the walk in a patio-size garden plot she tends in the backyard of her Carmel, Indiana, home. By interplanting and sowing consecutive crops, Linda gets her garden to deliver delicious taste and nutrition nearly year-round. She makes this yummy, healthful "pizza" at the peak of zucchini season.

PREP: 15 minutes
BAKE: at 350° about 35 minutes
STAND: 15 minutes
MAKES: 4 servings

1	medium-size onion, chopped (½ cup)
4	cups shredded zucchini (1 pound)
½	teaspoon salt
3	medium-size eggs or ¾ cup refrigerated or frozen egg product, thawed
½	cup finely shredded Parmesan cheese
⅓	cup all-purpose flour
1	teaspoon chopped fresh basil leaves
⅛	teaspoon black pepper
½	cup shredded mozzarella cheese (2 ounces)
1	medium-size zucchini, very thinly sliced crosswise (1¼ cups)
2	large tomatoes, sliced
	Sliced pitted ripe olives, for serving (optional)
	Finely shredded Parmesan cheese, for serving (optional)

1. Heat oven to 350°. Coat 12-inch pizza pan with nonstick cooking spray. Coat small skillet with nonstick cooking spray. Heat skillet over medium-high heat. Add onion; cook and stir about 3 minutes or until onion is tender but not brown. Set aside.

2. On large platter or shallow baking pan, spread shredded zucchini; sprinkle evenly with salt. Let stand for 15 minutes. Using paper towels, gently press excess moisture from zucchini.

3. In large bowl, beat together eggs, the ½ cup Parmesan cheese, flour, basil and pepper until combined. Stir in mozzarella cheese, shredded zucchini and onion until well combined. Pour into prepared pizza pan, spreading evenly.

4. Bake at 350° about 25 minutes or until top is light brown and eggs are set. Remove from oven. Arrange zucchini slices on top of baked mixture. Top with tomato slices. If desired, sprinkle with olives and/or additional Parmesan cheese. Bake 10 minutes.

Per serving: 233 cal., 11 g total fat (0 sat.) 183 mg chol., 554 mg sodium, 19 g carbo., 3 g fiber, 0 g pro.

Zippy Zucchini Pizza

Classy Cuban Sandwiches

The classic Cuban sandwich gets a touch of elegance and color in the form of tender fresh asparagus.

PREP: 20 minutes
COOK: 4 to 6 minutes
MAKES: 4 sandwiches

½	**pound fresh thin asparagus spears, trimmed**
2	**tablespoons water**
4	**hoagie buns or torpedo rolls, split**
2	**to 3 tablespoons coarse-grain mustard**
½	**pound sliced Swiss cheese**
6	**ounces thinly sliced cooked ham**
6	**ounces thinly sliced cooked turkey breast**
	Dill pickle slices
1	**tablespoon olive oil**

1. In microwave-safe 9-inch pie plate or shallow baking dish, combine asparagus and water; cover with vented plastic wrap. Microwave on HIGH for 3 minutes; drain and set aside.

2. Spread bottom halves of rolls with mustard. Top with cheese, asparagus, ham, turkey and pickle slices. Add roll tops.

3. In very large skillet or grill pan, heat oil over medium heat (or preheat covered electric indoor grill and brush with oil). Place sandwiches in skillet or grill pan or on electric grill (you may need to cook them in batches); cover sandwiches in skillet or grill pan with large, heavy plate and press gently (or close electric grill lid). Cook for 2 to 3 minutes per side (3 to 4 minutes total on covered grill) or until bread toasts and cheese melts.

Per sandwich: 799 cal., 35 g total fat (15 g sat.), 109 mg chol., 2,224 mg sodium, 79 g carbo., 5 g fiber, 42 g pro.

Beef Bunburgers

Sort of like sloppy joes, these loose-meat sandwiches are great for a weeknight family supper or for an informal gathering with friends. Serve them with veggies and dip, chips, and bar cookies or brownies.

PREP: 15 minutes
COOK: about 20 minutes
MAKES: 8 sandwiches

1½	pounds ground beef
1	medium-size onion, chopped
½	small green pepper, seeded and chopped (⅓ cup)
1	can (10¾ ounces) condensed tomato soup
1	tablespoon vinegar
1	teaspoon dry mustard
1	teaspoon poultry seasoning
½	teaspoon dried thyme
¼	teaspoon salt
8	hamburger buns, split and toasted

1. In large skillet, cook ground beef, onion and green pepper until beef is brown and onion is tender. Drain fat well.

2. Stir in soup, vinegar, dry mustard, poultry seasoning, thyme and salt. Bring to a boil. Reduce heat; simmer about 15 minutes or until desired consistency is achieved. Serve on hamburger buns.

Per sandwich: 364 cal., 19 g total fat (7 g sat.), 62 mg chol., 584 mg sodium, 28 g carbo., 2 g fiber, 20 g pro.

Roast Beef and Pepper Sandwiches

The full, hearty taste of beef is delicious paired with peppery flavors. These beef sandwiches get a triple dose: sweet peppers, a lip-tingling horseradish and Dijon mustard dressing and the peppery crunch of fresh watercress. Pictured on page 151.

PREP: 25 minutes
MAKES: 6 sandwiches

¼	cup light mayonnaise dressing or mayonnaise
2	tablespoons Dijon mustard
1½	teaspoons horseradish
6	(4- to 5-inch) ciabatta or other Italian rolls
2	cups fresh spinach
¾	pound thinly sliced cooked roast beef
6	ounces thinly sliced Monterey Jack cheese
1	cup drained roasted sweet red peppers, cut into ¼-inch-wide strips
2	cups fresh watercress, tough stems removed

1. In small bowl, combine mayonnaise dressing, Dijon mustard and horseradish. Using a serrated knife, slice bread in half horizontally.

2. To assemble, spread the roll bottoms with mayonnaise mixture. Top each with spinach, roast beef, cheese, red peppers, watercress and roll tops.

Per sandwich: 326 cal., 15 g total fat (7 g sat.), 60 mg chol., 543 mg sodium, 19 g carbo., 2 g fiber, 27 g pro.

Tuna Spinach Braid

PREP: 25 minutes
BAKE: at 375° for 18 to 20 minutes
MAKES: 4 to 6 servings

- 1 **package (10 ounces) frozen chopped spinach, thawed and squeezed dry**
- 1 **can (9¼ ounces) chunk white tuna (water pack), drained and flaked**
- 1 **cup low-fat ricotta cheese or cream-style cottage cheese, drained**
- ½ **cup grated Parmesan cheese**
- 1 **clove garlic, finely chopped**
- 1 **package (8) refrigerated crescent rolls**
- 3 **thick slices provolone cheese**

1. Heat oven to 375°. In medium-size bowl, combine spinach, tuna, ricotta cheese, Parmesan cheese and garlic.

2. Unroll and separate crescent dough into 4 rectangles. On baking sheet or shallow baking pan, place rectangles together, overlapping edges slightly, for 14×10-inch rectangle. Firmly press edges and perforations together to seal.

3. Spread spinach mixture in 3½-inch-wide strip lengthwise down center of dough. Top with provolone, cutting cheese as necessary to cover spinach mixture.

4. Make cuts in dough at 1-inch intervals on both long sides of rectangle just to edge of filling. Fold dough strips diagonally over filling, overlapping strips and alternating from side to side to produce a braided appearance.

5. Bake at 375° for 18 to 20 minutes or until golden. Cut into serving-size pieces. Serve warm.

Per serving: 480 cal., 27 g total fat (11 g sat.), 56 mg chol., 1,139 mg sodium, 29 g carbo., 3 g fiber, 34 g pro.

Mu Shu-Style Pork Wraps

Flour tortillas stand in for the traditional pancakes in this super-simple wrap.

PREP: 10 minutes
BAKE: at 350° for 10 minutes
COOK: 6 to 7 minutes
MAKES: 4 wraps

- 4 **(10-inch) flour tortillas**
- 1 **teaspoon dark Asian sesame oil**
- ¾ **pound lean boneless pork, cut into bite-size strips**
- 2 **cups frozen stir-fry vegetables (any combination)**
- ¼ **cup bottled plum or hoisin sauce**

1. Heat oven to 350°. Wrap tortillas tightly in foil. Bake at 350° for 10 minutes to soften. (Or wrap tortillas in white microwave-safe paper towels; microwave on HIGH for 15 to 30 seconds or until tortillas soften.)

2. In large skillet, heat sesame oil over medium-high heat. Add pork strips; stir-fry about 3 minutes. Add stir-fry vegetables. Cook and stir for 3 to 4 minutes or until vegetables are crisp-tender.

3. Spread each tortilla with 1 tablespoon plum sauce; place one-fourth of meat mixture just below center of each tortilla. Fold bottom edge of each tortilla up and over filling. Fold in sides until they meet; roll up over filling.

Per wrap: 296 cal., 8 g total fat (2 g sat.), 53 mg chol., 325 mg sodium, 32 g carbo., 1 g fiber, 22 g pro.

Five-Spice Steak Wraps

Chinese five-spice powder is a combination of ground fennel, cloves, star anise, cinnamon and Szechuan peppercorns. It's fairly widely available—look for it in the spice aisle of your supermarket.

PREP: 20 minutes
COOK: 3 to 4 minutes
MAKES: 4 wraps

1	boneless beef round steak (¾ pound)
2	cups packaged shredded cabbage with carrot (coleslaw mix)
¼	cup thin strips red sweet pepper and/or green pepper
¼	cup thin strips carrot
¼	cup chopped fresh chives
2	tablespoons rice vinegar
½	teaspoon dark Asian sesame oil
½	teaspoon five-spice powder
¼	teaspoon salt
¼	cup plain low-fat yogurt or light sour cream
4	(8-inch) flour tortillas

1. If desired, partially freeze steak for easier slicing. Trim fat from steak. Thinly slice steak across grain into bite-size strips. Set aside.

2. In medium bowl, combine coleslaw mix, sweet pepper, carrot and chives. In small bowl, combine rice vinegar and sesame oil. Pour vinegar mixture over coleslaw mixture; toss to coat.

3. Season steak with five-spice powder and salt. Coat unheated large nonstick skillet with nonstick cooking spray. Heat skillet over medium-high heat. Add steak strips; stir-fry for 3 to 4 minutes or until brown. Remove from heat.

4. To assemble, spread 1 tablespoon yogurt along one edge of each tortilla. Top with steak strips. Stir coleslaw mixture; spoon over steak. Fold in sides of tortillas. Roll starting from edge with filling. If desired, secure with toothpicks or short skewers.

Per wrap: 237 cal., 7 g total fat (2 g sat.), 51 mg chol., 329 mg sodium, 20 g carbo., 2 g fiber, 22 g pro.

Pizza by the Yard

PREP: 20 minutes
BROIL: about 1 minute
BAKE: at 350° for 8 to 10 minutes
MAKES: 6 servings

1	loaf (16 ounces) unsliced French bread
1	pound lean ground beef
1	can (6 ounces) tomato paste
¼	cup water
¼	cup chopped pitted ripe olives
2	scallions, trimmed and thinly sliced
½	teaspoon dried oregano
½	teaspoon salt
⅓	cup grated Parmesan cheese
2	medium-size tomatoes, sliced
1	medium-size green pepper, seeded and cut into rings
1	cup shredded American cheese

1. Heat broiler. Using a serrated knife, cut bread in half horizontally. Place bread halves, cut sides up, on unheated rack of broiler pan. Broil 4 inches from heat 1 minute or until lightly toasted. Transfer to large baking sheet; set aside. Heat oven to 350°.

2. In large skillet, cook ground beef until meat is brown. Drain off fat. Stir in tomato paste, water, olives, scallions, oregano, salt and ⅛ teaspoon ground black pepper. Cook and stir over medium heat until heated through. Remove from heat; stir in Parmesan cheese.

3. To assemble, top bread halves evenly with ground beef mixture, tomato slices, green pepper rings and cheese. Bake at 350° for 8 to 10 minutes or until cheese melts. Cut into serving-size pieces. Serve immediately.

Per serving: 545 cal., 26 g total fat (11 g sat.), 81 mg chol., 1,413 mg sodium, 49 g carbo., 5 g fiber, 29 g pro.

Pizza Margherita

The story goes that this most classic of Neapolitan pizzas was created in honor of the Italian queen, Margherita, in 1889. It features the colors of the Italian flag: red, white and green.

PREP: 10 minutes
BAKE: at 425° about 15 minutes
MAKES: 4 pizzas

4	(6- to 7-inch) baked pizza crusts (such as Boboli)
1½	cups shredded pizza-blend cheese (6 ounces)
4	plum tomatoes or 2 medium tomatoes, thinly sliced
2	to 3 teaspoons olive oil or vegetable oil
¼	cup pine nuts (optional)
½	cup finely shredded fresh basil leaves

1. Heat oven to 425°. On very large baking sheet, place pizza crusts. Bake at 425° for 5 minutes. Remove from oven; sprinkle with cheese and top with tomato slices. Drizzle tomato slices with oil. If desired, sprinkle with pine nuts. Top with basil.

2. Bake at 425° about 10 minutes or until heated through. Serve immediately.

Per pizza: 572 cal., 21 g total fat (10 g sat.), 30 mg chol., 1,110 mg sodium, 69 g carbo., 3 g fiber, 25 g pro.

Roasted Garlic-Sausage Pizza

Garlic mellows considerably when it's roasted. The sugars caramelize and sweeten—so each creamy bite is aromatic and delicious, not bracing.

PREP: 25 minutes
BAKE: at 425° for 25 to 35 minutes for garlic;
for 14 to 16 minutes for pizzas
MAKES: 8 to 12 servings

	Cornmeal
2	**heads garlic**
1	**teaspoon olive oil**
1	**pound bulk Italian sausage**
2	**cups sliced fresh mushrooms**
2	**tubes (13.8 ounces each) refrigerated pizza crust dough**
1	**can (8 ounces) pizza sauce**
1	**medium-size green pepper, seeded and cut into thin bite-size strips**
2	**medium-size plum tomatoes, sliced and quartered**
2	**cups shredded provolone cheese (8 ounces)**

1. Heat oven to 425°. Grease 2 large baking sheets; sprinkle with cornmeal. Set aside. To roast garlic, use sharp knife to cut off top ½ inch from each garlic head, leaving garlic heads whole but exposing individual cloves. Place garlic, cut sides up, in custard cups or small casserole. Drizzle with olive oil. Cover with foil and bake at 425° for 25 to 35 minutes or until cloves feel soft when pressed. Set aside until cool enough to handle. Squeeze roasted garlic cloves from skins, leaving cloves intact. Discard skins.*

2. In large skillet, cook sausage and mushrooms until sausage is brown. Drain off fat.

3. Unroll dough. Transfer each dough to prepared baking sheet. Bake at 425° about 8 minutes or until light brown.

4. Spread each crust with half of sauce; top with half of sausage mixture, half of garlic cloves, half of sweet pepper strips, half of tomatoes and half of cheese. Bake for 6 to 8 minutes or until cheese melts. Cut into pieces.

*Note: If desired, roast the garlic up to 3 days ahead and store in the refrigerator until ready to use.

Per serving: 530 cal., 26 g total fat (11 g sat.), 59 mg chol., 996 mg sodium, 46 g carbo., 3 g fiber, 24 g pro.

Chapter 9

Save Room

Sweet Endings

This time-tested collection of fruit desserts, indulgent brownies and heavenly-tasting bars, cakes, cookies, pies and puddings will satisfy your sweet tooth and put a smile on your face.

Almond Squares

Mom's Special Ice Cream Cookie Dessert

Mom's Special Ice Cream Cookie Dessert

Marge Mitchell of Portland, Oregon, says her family loves vanilla ice cream with chocolate sauce and nuts. They also love chocolate chip cookies. She put all of those favorite treats together to enter a Nestlé-sponsored cooking contest and won $1,000, which bought a new refrigerator and freezer. She keeps them well stocked with yummy desserts.

PREP: 1 hour
BAKE: at 375° for 8 to 10 minutes
FREEZE: 4 to 24 hours
STAND: 10 to 15 minutes
MAKES: 16 servings

- 1 **roll (18 ounces) refrigerated chocolate chip cookie dough**

Sugared Nuts:
- 1 **cup chopped walnuts**
- 2 **tablespoons (¼ stick) butter, melted**
- 1 **tablespoon light-brown sugar**

Chocolate Sauce:
- 1 **can (12 ounces) evaporated milk**
- 1 **cup semisweet chocolate chips**
- 1 **cup confectioners' sugar**
- 2 **ounces unsweetened chocolate, chopped**
- 2 **tablespoons (¼ stick) butter**
- 1 **tablespoon vanilla extract**
- ½ **gallon vanilla ice cream, softened**

1. Bake cookie dough following package directions. Cool cookies and chop into small pieces (you should have about 5 cups).

2. Sugared Nuts: Heat oven to 375°. Grease 9×9×2-inch baking pan. Combine nuts, the 2 tablespoons melted butter and brown sugar. Spread into prepared pan. Bake at 375° for 8 to 10 minutes or until nuts are toasted. Stir well. Cool in pan on wire rack.

3. Chocolate Sauce: In saucepan, combine milk, chocolate chips, confectioners' sugar, unsweetened chocolate and 2 tablespoons butter. Cook over medium heat 5 to 7 minutes or until thickened, stirring often. Stir in vanilla. Cool completely.

4. To assemble, wrap outside of 9-inch springform pan with foil. Sprinkle one-third of chopped cookies on bottom of pan. Top with half of the ice cream and half of the chocolate sauce. Combine remaining cookies and nut mixture. Sprinkle half of the cookie-walnut mixture over the chocolate sauce. Set aside 2 tablespoons of the remaining chocolate sauce. Top mixture in pan with remaining ice cream, chocolate sauce and cookie-walnut mixture. Drizzle reserved chocolate sauce over top. Freeze 4 to 24 hours. To serve, let stand at room temperature for 10 to 15 minutes. Remove side of pan. Cut into wedges.

Per serving: 485 cal., 29 g total fat (13 g sat.), 48 mg chol., 205 mg sodium, 53 g carbo., 3 g fiber, 7 g pro.

Sour Cream Lemon Pie

You might say that participants in RAGBRAI, the oldest organized bike ride in the country, are really just pedaling for pie. Iowa's best bakers pull out all the stops to bake for the thousands of cyclists who bike across their state each summer. This meringue-topped beauty from Ione Burhnam, of Washington, Iowa, was deemed one of the best.

PREP: 25 minutes
BAKE: at 350° for 18 minutes
COOL: 1 hour
CHILL: 3 to 6 hours
MAKES: 8 servings

3	egg whites

Lemon Filling:

1	cup sugar
3	tablespoons cornstarch
1	cup milk
4	tablespoons (½ stick) butter, cut up
3	egg yolks, beaten
¼	cup lemon juice
1	cup sour cream
1	teaspoon finely shredded lemon peel

Meringue:

½	teaspoon vanilla extract
¼	teaspoon cream of tartar
6	tablespoons sugar
1	baked 9-inch pastry shell

1. In large bowl, allow egg whites to stand at room temperature 30 minutes.

2. Lemon Filling: Heat oven to 350°. In saucepan, combine 1 cup sugar, 2 tablespoons of the cornstarch and a pinch of salt. Add milk and butter. Cook and stir over medium heat until thickened and bubbly; cook and stir 2 minutes. Gradually stir thickened mixture into egg yolks; return to pan. Cook and stir 2 minutes. Stir in lemon juice. Combine sour cream, lemon peel and remaining 1 tablespoon cornstarch. Gradually stir ½ cup hot mixture into sour cream mixture. Return all to pan; cook and stir until mixture comes to a boil. Remove from heat; cover and keep warm.

3. Meringue: Beat egg whites, vanilla and cream of tartar about 1 minute or until soft peaks form. Gradually add the 6 tablespoons sugar, 1 tablespoon at a time, beating on high speed 4 minutes more or until mixture forms stiff peaks and sugar dissolves.

4. Pour hot filling into pastry shell. Spread meringue over hot filling, carefully sealing to edge of pastry. Bake at 350° for 18 minutes. Cool on rack 1 hour. Chill 3 to 6 hours. Cover for longer storage.

Per serving: 492 cal., 28 g total fat (12 g sat.), 111 mg chol., 243 mg sodium, 56 g carbo., 1 g fiber, 7 g pro.

Sour Cream Lemon Pie

Oatmeal Chocolate Chip Cookies

You can have your cookie and eat it too—these chewy chocolate chip cookies are loaded with fiber-rich oats and prunes.

PREP: 15 minutes
BAKE: at 375° about 15 minutes per batch
MAKES: 48 cookies

2½	cups all-purpose flour
2	teaspoons baking powder
¼	teaspoon baking soda
½	teaspoon salt
1	cup (2 sticks) unsalted butter, softened
1	cup packed light-brown sugar
½	cup granulated sugar
1	teaspoon vanilla extract
1	egg
1	cup quick oats
¾	pound pitted prunes, chopped
1	cup chopped walnuts
1	package (12 ounces) semisweet chocolate chips
	Confectioners' sugar (optional)

1. Heat oven to 375°. In large bowl, combine flour, baking powder, baking soda and salt. In a second large bowl, cream butter with an electric mixer on medium speed. Add brown sugar and granulated sugar and beat until fluffy. Beat in vanilla and egg. Add flour mixture and mix well. Stir in oats, prunes, nuts and chips.

2. Drop dough by rounded tablespoons onto cookie sheets. Bake at 375° about 15 minutes or until lightly browned around edges. Transfer cookies to wire racks and cool completely. Repeat with remaining dough.

3. If desired, just before serving, sprinkle cooled cookies with confectioners' sugar.

Per cookie: 158 cal., 8 g total fat (4 g sat.), 15 mg chol., 51 mg sodium, 22 g carbo., 1 g fiber, 1 g pro.

Chocolate Goody Bars

These irresistible bars feature the best of both worlds: a soft, fudge-brownie foundation topped off with a crunchy peanut butter-and-chocolate crown.

PREP: 20 minutes
BAKE: at 350° for 28 to 30 minutes
CHILL: 30 minutes
MAKES: 36 bars

1	box (19.8 ounces) fudge brownie mix
½	cup vegetable oil
2	eggs
¼	cup water
1	can (1 pound) prepared vanilla frosting
¾	cup chopped peanuts
3	cups crisp rice cereal
1	cup creamy peanut butter
1	package (12 ounces) semisweet chocolate chips

1. Heat oven to 350°. Grease 13×9×2-inch baking pan. In large bowl, combine brownie mix, vegetable oil, eggs and water until well mixed. Spread mixture in prepared pan.

2. Bake at 350° for 28 to 30 minutes or until toothpick inserted 2 inches from side of pan comes out clean. Cool completely on wire rack.

3. Spread frosting over brownie. Sprinkle with peanuts. Cover and refrigerate.

4. Meanwhile, in medium-size bowl, place rice cereal. In small saucepan, combine peanut butter and chocolate chips. Heat and stir over low heat until chocolate melts. Pour over cereal. Stir to coat evenly. Spread cereal mixture over frosting. Cover and refrigerate until cereal layer is set. Cut into 36 bars. Store, covered, in refrigerator.

Per bar: 261 cal., 14 g total fat (2 g sat.), 12 mg chol., 150 mg sodium, 33 g carbo., 1 g fiber, 4 g pro.

Chocolate Goody Bars

Pecan Shortbread Raspberry Cookies

Pecan Shortbread Raspberry Cookies

A window in the top of these buttery shortbread cookies reveals an eye-catching dollop of raspberry jam.

PREP: 40 minutes
BAKE: at 350° for 7 to 9 minutes per batch
CHILL: 1 to 2 hours
MAKES: about 40

1	cup (2 sticks) butter, softened
⅔	cup granulated sugar
1	teaspoon vanilla extract
½	teaspoon almond extract
2	cups all-purpose flour
1	cup ground pecans
	Confectioners' sugar
⅓	cup seedless raspberry preserves

1. In large bowl, beat butter with electric mixer on medium to high speed 30 seconds. Add granulated sugar, vanilla and almond extract; beat until fluffy, scraping bowl often. Beat in flour and pecans until combined. Wrap dough in plastic wrap; refrigerate for 1 to 2 hours or until dough is easy to handle.

2. Heat oven to 350°. On floured surface, roll dough, half at a time, to ⅛-inch thickness. Using 2-inch scalloped round cookie cutter, cut rounds from dough. Place rounds 1 inch apart on ungreased cookie sheets. Using a 1-inch scalloped round cutter, cut centers from half of unbaked cookies. Remove centers; reroll dough to make more cookies. Bake at 350° for 7 to 9 minutes or until edges are firm and bottoms are light brown. Transfer cookies to wire rack to cool completely.

3. To assemble, sift confectioners' sugar over tops of cookies with holes. Spread about ½ teaspoon preserves onto bottom of each cookie without hole. Top with a cookie with a hole, sugar side up.

Per cookie: 100 cal., 6 g total fat (3 g sat.), 12 mg chol., 47 mg sodium, 10 g carbo., 0 g fiber, 1 g pro.

Pumpkin-Nut Cookies

PREP: 30 minutes
BAKE: at 350° for 12 to 15 minutes per batch
MAKES: 72 cookies

Cookies:

1	cup (2 sticks) butter, softened
2	cups granulated sugar
1	can (15 ounces) pumpkin
2	teaspoons baking powder
2	teaspoons ground cinnamon
1	teaspoon salt
¾	teaspoon ground nutmeg
½	teaspoon baking soda
½	teaspoon ground allspice
2	eggs
1	tablespoon vanilla extract
4	cups all-purpose flour
1½	cups chopped pecans

Icing:

4	cups confectioners' sugar
¼	cup milk
1	teaspoon vanilla extract

1. Cookies: Heat oven to 350°. Grease cookie sheets. In large bowl, beat butter with an electric mixer on medium speed for 30 seconds. Add granulated sugar, pumpkin, baking powder, cinnamon, salt, nutmeg, soda and allspice. Beat mixture until combined. Beat in eggs and vanilla. Beat in as much of the flour as you can with the mixer. Stir in remaining flour. Stir in pecans.

2. Drop dough by rounded teaspoons 1 inch apart onto prepared cookie sheets. Bake at 350° for 12 to 15 minutes or until the edges are golden. Transfer cookies to wire rack and cool completely.

3. Icing: In medium-size mixing bowl, combine confectioners' sugar, milk and vanilla. Stir in additional milk, if necessary to reach desired spreading consistency. Spread icing over cookies.

Per cookie: 87 cal., 4 g total fat (2 g sat.), 13 mg chol., 77 mg sodium, 12 g carbo., 0 g fiber, 1 g pro.

Chocolate Zucchini Bars

Shredded zucchini makes these rich, cinnamon-infused bars moist and delicious.

PREP: 15 minutes
BAKE: at 325° for 30 to 35 minutes
MAKES: 16 bars

1½	cups all-purpose flour
1½	tablespoons unsweetened cocoa powder
½	teaspoon baking soda
½	teaspoon ground cinnamon
¼	teaspoon baking powder
¼	cup solid vegetable shortening
¼	cup vegetable oil
¾	cup sugar
1	egg
¼	cup sour cream
½	teaspoon vanilla extract
1	cup grated zucchini
¾	cup mini semisweet chocolate chips
⅓	cup crushed walnuts

1. Heat oven to 325°. Coat 13×9×2-inch baking pan with nonstick cooking spray.

2. In large bowl, whisk together flour, cocoa powder, baking soda, cinnamon and baking powder.

3. In another large bowl, beat shortening, oil, sugar and egg with an electric mixer on low speed until smooth. Beat in sour cream and vanilla, then flour mixture. Beat on medium speed for 2 minutes. Fold in zucchini and chocolate chips.

4. Spread batter into prepared pan. Sprinkle with walnuts. Bake at 325° for 30 to 35 minutes or until toothpick inserted in center comes out clean. Cool in pan on wire rack. To serve, cut into bars.

Per bar: 227 cal., 12 g total fat (4 g sat.), 15 mg chol., 52 mg sodium, 27 g carbo., 1 g fiber, 2 g pro.

Waldorf Squares

PREP: 15 minutes
BAKE: at 350° for 40 minutes
MAKES: 48 squares

Cookie Base:

½	cup (1 stick) cold unsalted butter
1	cup all-purpose flour

Filling:

2	eggs
½	cup packed light-brown sugar
1	cup chopped walnuts or pecans
1	cup sweetened flake coconut
2	tablespoons imitation maple syrup
1	teaspoon vanilla extract
⅓	cup all-purpose flour
½	teaspoon baking powder

Frosting:

6	tablespoons (¾ stick) unsalted butter
1	box (1 pound) confectioners' sugar
¼	cup heavy cream
1½	teaspoons vanilla extract

1. Cookie Base: Heat oven to 350°. Coat 13×9×2-inch baking pan with nonstick cooking spray. Using pastry blender, cut the ½ cup butter into the 1 cup flour. Press mixture evenly onto bottom of prepared pan. Bake at 350° for 15 minutes. Cool in pan.

2. Filling: In bowl, beat eggs and brown sugar until combined. Stir in nuts, coconut, maple syrup and the 1 teaspoon vanilla. In bowl, combine the ⅓ cup flour, 1 teaspoon salt and baking powder. Fold flour mixture into egg mixture. Spread over cooled cookie base. Bake at 350° 25 minutes. Cool.

3. Frosting: Beat the 6 tablespoons butter on medium speed for 30 seconds. Gradually add half of the confectioners' sugar. Beat in 2 tablespoons of the cream and the 1½ teaspoons vanilla. Blend in remaining sugar and enough cream for a good consistency. Frost; let set up to 30 minutes.

Per serving: 126 cal., 6 g total fat (3 g sat.), 19 mg chol., 16 mg sodium, 16 g carbo., 0 g fiber, 1 g pro.

Strawberry Delight

When it's the height of peach season, this delightful dessert can also be made with 3 cups of sliced fresh peaches and peach-flavored gelatin.

PREP: 20 minutes
BAKE: at 350° about 20 minutes
COOL: 30 minutes
CHILL: 4 to 24 hours
MAKES: 15 servings

Crust:
1½	cups all-purpose flour
¾	cup (1½ sticks) butter, melted
¾	cup chopped pecans

Filling:
2	cups confectioners' sugar
1	package (8 ounces) cream cheese, softened
1	container (8 ounces) frozen whipped dessert topping, thawed
3	cups sliced fresh strawberries

Strawberry Topping:
1	cup granulated sugar
¼	cup all-purpose flour
3	tablespoons strawberry-flavored gelatin
1	cup water
	Frozen whipped dessert topping, thawed, for garnish (optional)

1. Crust: Heat oven to 350°. In medium-size bowl, combine the 1½ cups flour and melted butter; stir in pecans. Pat evenly onto bottom of 13×9×2-inch baking dish. Bake at 350° about 20 minutes or until golden brown around edges. Cool on wire rack.

2. Filling: In large bowl, beat confectioners' sugar and cream cheese with an electric mixer on medium speed until combined. Add the 8 ounces whipped topping by spoonfuls; beat until smooth. Spread mixture over cooled crust. Arrange strawberries on top. Cover and refrigerate while preparing top layer.

3. Strawberry Topping: In medium-size saucepan, combine granulated sugar, the ¼ cup flour and strawberry-flavored gelatin. Stir in water. Cook and stir until thickened and bubbly; cook and stir for 1 minute more. Remove from heat. Cover surface with plastic wrap; set aside to cool.

4. Spoon cooled gelatin mixture over berries. Cover and refrigerate for 4 to 24 hours. Cut into squares to serve. If desired, garnish each serving with additional whipped topping.

Per serving: 389 cal., 22 g total fat (12 g sat.), 43 mg chol., 152 mg sodium, 46 g carbo., 2 g fiber, 4 g pro.

Peach Upside-Down Cake

Make this homestyle dessert at the peak of peach season, in late July or August. It's best served warm—and be sure to get all the caramellike sauce from the bottom of the pan after you've turned the cake onto the serving plate.

PREP: 30 minutes
BAKE: at 325° for 40 to 45 minutes
COOL: 10 minutes
MAKES: 10 servings

4	tablespoons (½ stick) butter
⅔	cup packed light-brown sugar
2	cups peeled, pitted and sliced fresh peaches or frozen unsweetened peach slices*
½	cup chopped pecans
4	eggs, separated
1	teaspoon vanilla extract
1	cup granulated sugar
2	tablespoons butter, melted and cooled
1	cup cake flour
1	teaspoon baking powder
¼	teaspoon salt
	Whipped cream (optional)
	Chopped pecans (optional)

1. Heat oven to 325°. In 10-inch nonstick ovenproof skillet, melt the 4 tablespoons butter. Remove from heat. Stir in brown sugar; spread evenly in pan. Arrange peaches on sugar mixture; sprinkle with the ½ cup pecans.

2. In large bowl, beat egg whites and vanilla with electric mixer on medium speed until soft peaks form. Slowly add granulated sugar, beating until stiff peaks form.

3. In small bowl, combine egg yolks and 2 tablespoons melted butter; stir into egg white mixture. In another small bowl, sift together flour, baking powder and salt. Sprinkle about one-fourth of the flour mixture at a time over egg mixture; gently stir in by hand. Spoon batter over peaches in skillet, spreading evenly.

4. Bake at 325° for 40 to 45 minutes or until toothpick inserted near center comes out clean. Cool in pan on wire rack for 10 minutes.

5. Loosen edge; carefully invert onto serving plate. Remove skillet. Serve warm. If desired, top with whipped cream and additional pecans.

*Note: Thaw frozen peaches; drain well.

Per serving: 331 cal., 13 g total fat (6 g sat.), 105 mg chol., 203 mg sodium, 51 g carbo., 2 g fiber, 4 g pro.

Crescent Fruit Pizza

Use whatever fruits are in season to top this sweetie pie. That means fresh berries in early and mid-summer, peaches in late summer and sliced ripe pears in the fall.

PREP: 35 minutes
BAKE: at 375° for 11 to 13 minutes
CHILL: 1 to 3 hours
MAKES: 8 servings

1	tube (8 ounces) refrigerated crescent rolls
1	tablespoon butter or margarine, melted
½	teaspoon almond extract
4	teaspoons sugar
1	box (3.4 ounces) instant vanilla pudding mix
1½	cups milk
1	teaspoon finely shredded orange peel
¼	container (8 ounces) frozen whipped dessert topping, thawed (1 cup)
3	cups fresh fruit (such as blueberries, sliced kiwifruit, sliced strawberries, raspberries and/or peeled peach slices)

1. Heat oven to 375°F. Press rolls into bottom of 12-inch pizza pan or 13×9×2-inch baking pan. In small bowl, combine butter and almond extract; brush over dough. Sprinkle with sugar.

2. Bake at 375° for 11 to 13 minutes or until golden. Cool completely in pan on wire rack

3. In medium-size bowl, beat pudding mix and milk with electric mixer on low speed for 1 minute. Stir in orange peel. Cover and refrigerate for 10 minutes. Fold in dessert topping.

4. Spread pudding mixture evenly over crust. Arrange fruit over pudding. Cover and refrigerate for 1 to 3 hours before serving.

Per serving: 236 cal., 10 g total fat (4 g sat.), 7 mg chol., 430 mg sodium, 35 g carbo., 2 g fiber, 4 g pro.

Easy Fruit Cobbler

This old-fashioned favorite is best served warm from the oven. Add a scoop of vanilla ice cream or a spoonful of fresh cream an extra treat.

PREP: 15 minutes
BAKE: at 400° for 20 to 25 minutes
MAKES: 6 servings

6	cups desired frozen fruit, such as sliced peaches and/or raspberries or blueberries, thawed*
¼	cup granulated sugar
2	tablespoons quick-cooking tapioca
2	cups packaged biscuit mix
2	tablespoons sugar
½	cup milk
	Cinnamon-sugar (optional)

1. Heat oven to 400°. In large bowl, stir together undrained fruit, the ¼ cup granulated sugar, and the tapioca. Transfer fruit mixture to a 2-quart square baking dish.

2. In medium bowl, stir together biscuit mix, the 2 tablespoons sugar, and the milk until combined. Using a spoon, drop topping into six mounds on top of fruit mixture. If desired, sprinkle mounds lightly with cinnamon-sugar.

3. Bake at 400° for 20 to 25 minutes or until filling is bubbly and topping is golden. Let cool in dish on wire rack about 1 hour. Serve warm.

*Note: Thaw fruit overnight in the refrigerator.

Per serving: 152 cal., 3 g total fat (1 g sat.), 1 mg chol., 252 mg sodium, 31 g carbo., 2 g fiber, 3 g pro.

Black Forest Bread Pudding

Germany's Black Forest cake features the flavors of rich, dark chocolate and sweet and fruity cherries. This recipe has that fetching combination in a simple and satisfying baked pudding that can be assembled up to a day ahead of baking.

PREP: 30 minutes
CHILL: 2 hours to overnight
BAKE: at 325° for 70 to 80 minutes
COOL: 45 minutes
MAKES: 16 to 20 servings

5	tablespoons butter, softened
12	ounces black rye bread, sliced ½ inch thick
1	package (12 to 16 ounces) frozen pitted dark sweet cherries
2	packages (12 ounces each) semisweet chocolate chips
½	teaspoon ground cinnamon
3¼	cups heavy cream
¾	cup sugar
8	eggs
½	teaspoon almond extract
	Whipped cream, for serving (optional)
	Sliced almonds, toasted, for serving (optional)

1. Butter 13×9×2-inch baking dish with some of the butter; spread remaining butter on bread slices. Place bread slices in baking dish, overlapping as necessary to fit. Sprinkle with frozen cherries, half of the chocolate pieces and cinnamon.

2. In medium-size saucepan, combine remaining chocolate pieces, 1 cup of the heavy cream and sugar. Heat and stir just until chocolate melts. Gradually stir in remaining cream. In very large bowl, beat eggs; stir in melted chocolate mixture and almond extract. Slowly pour over bread in dish (dish will be very full). Cover and refrigerate for 2 hours or overnight.

3. Heat oven to 325°. Uncover baking dish and place on foil-lined baking sheet. Bake at 325° for 70 to 80 minutes or until an instant-read thermometer inserted in center registers 160°. Cool on wire rack at least 45 minutes. Serve warm. If desired, top with whipped cream and almonds.

Per serving: 546 cal., 38 g total fat (22 g sat.), 183 mg chol., 229 mg sodium, 51 g carbo., 4 g fiber, 8 g pro.

Apple-Walnut Bake

Granny Smith apples are a perfect choice for this autumnal dessert. They have a wonderful tart taste and hold up well when cooked.

PREP: 25 minutes
BAKE: at 350° for 30 to 35 minutes
MAKES: 8 servings

Cinnamon Butter:

4	tablespoons (½ stick) butter
1	cup confectioners' sugar
1	tablespoon milk
1	teaspoon vanilla extract
½	teaspoon ground cinnamon

Apple Bake:

1	cup packed light-brown sugar
¾	cup all-purpose flour
1½	teaspoons baking powder
¼	teaspoon salt
¼	teaspoon ground cinnamon
2	eggs, lightly beaten
1½	teaspoons vanilla extract
2	cups peeled, cored and chopped tart cooking apples
¾	cup chopped walnuts

1. Cinnamon Butter: In small bowl, beat butter with electric mixer on medium to high speed for 30 seconds. Add confectioners' sugar, milk, the 1 teaspoon vanilla and the ½ teaspoon cinnamon. Beat until combined. Cover and refrigerate until firm.

2. Apple Bake: Heat oven to 350°. Grease 9-inch pie plate. In medium-size bowl, combine brown sugar, flour, baking powder, salt and the ¼ teaspoon cinnamon. Add eggs and vanilla; mix well. Stir in apples and walnuts. Spoon mixture into pie plate.

3. Bake at 350° for 30 to 35 minutes or until top is brown and firm. Cut into wedges. Serve warm with Cinnamon Butter.

Per serving: 365 cal., 15 g total fat (4 g sat.), 69 mg chol., 192 mg sodium, 55 g carbo., 2 g fiber, 5 g pro.

Hummingbird Cake

PREP: 25 minutes
BAKE: at 350° about 28 minutes
MAKES: 16 servings

Cake:

- 3 cups all-purpose flour
- 2 cups sugar
- 1 teaspoon baking soda
- 1 teaspoon ground cinnamon
- 3 large eggs, lightly beaten
- ¾ cup vegetable oil
- 1 cup chopped pecans
- 2 large ripe bananas, mashed
- 1 can (8 ounces) crushed pineapple, undrained
- 1½ teaspoons vanilla extract

Frosting:

- 1 package (8 ounces) cream cheese, softened
- ½ cup (1 stick) unsalted butter, softened
- 1 box (1 pound) confectioners' sugar
- 1 teaspoon vanilla extract

1. Cake: Heat oven to 350°. Butter and flour two 9-inch cake pans. In bowl, mix flour, sugar, baking soda, 1 teaspoon salt and cinnamon. Add eggs and oil. Stir just until dry ingredients are moistened. Stir in pecans, bananas, pineapple and the 1½ teaspoons vanilla. Evenly divide batter between prepared pans. Bake at 350° about 28 minutes or until cake tests done. Cool in pan on rack for 15 minutes. Turn out; cool completely.

2. Frosting: In bowl, beat cream cheese and butter with electric mixer until creamy. Gradually beat in confectioners' sugar. Beat in the 1 teaspoon vanilla.

3. To assemble, place one cake layer on serving plate. Spread about 1 cup frosting over top. Place second layer on top. Frost top and sides of cake. Refrigerate for at least 1 hour before serving.

Per serving: 572 cal., 27 g total fat (9 g sat.), 71 mg chol., 136 mg sodium, 80 g carbo., 2 g fiber, 4 g pro.

Family Cheesecake

This simple and lovely cheesecake is a blank slate. You can serve it as is, or top it with fruit, a drizzle of caramel or chocolate ice cream topping or a sprinkling of chopped toffee.

PREP: 10 minutes
BAKE: at 350° about 1 hour
COOL: 3 hours
MAKES: 16 servings

- 4 packages (8 ounces each) cream cheese, softened
- 1½ cups sugar
- ½ cup cornstarch
- 1 cup (2 sticks) unsalted butter, softened
- 2 cups heavy cream
- 6 eggs

1. Heat oven to 350°. Coat 10-inch springform pan with nonstick cooking spray. Wrap outside of pan with foil. In large bowl, beat cream cheese with an electric mixer on medium speed until smooth. Add sugar, then cornstarch, butter, cream and eggs, beating well after each addition. Pour into prepared pan. Place in another pan filled with 1 inch water.

2. Bake at 350° about 1 hour or until golden brown. Cool in pan on wire rack. Once cheesecake cools (about 3 hours), remove side of pan, cover and refrigerate until ready to serve.

Per serving: 518 cal., 44 g total fat (27 g sat.), 213 mg chol., 207 mg sodium, 25 g carbo., 0 g fiber, 7 g pro.

Almond Squares

Pictured on page 167.

PREP: 25 minutes
BAKE: at 350° for 20 to 25 minutes
BROIL: about 1 minute
MAKES: 32 bars

2	eggs
1	cup sugar
1	cup (2 sticks) butter, melted
1	cup all-purpose flour
½	cup (1 stick) butter
½	cup sugar
½	cup sliced almonds
1	tablespoon all-purpose flour
1	tablespoon milk

1. Heat oven to 350°. Grease and lightly flour 13×9×2-inch baking pan. In medium-size bowl, beat eggs and the 1 cup sugar with electric mixer on medium speed about 8 minutes or until thick and lemon-colored. Stir in the 1 cup melted butter and the 1 cup flour. Pour into prepared pan.

2. Bake at 350° for 20 to 25 minutes or until wooden toothpick inserted near center comes out clean and edges begin to pull away from pan.

3. Meanwhile, in small saucepan, combine the ½ cup butter, the ½ cup sugar, almonds, the 1 tablespoon flour and milk. Cook and stir over medium heat until mixture comes to a boil. Remove from heat.

4. Heat broiler. Adjust oven rack so top of pan is 3 to 4 inches from heat. Spoon almond mixture over hot crust. Broil about 1 minute or until golden, watching carefully to avoid burning. Let cool in pan on wire rack. Cut into bars.

Per bar: 147 cal., 11 g total fat (6 g sat.), 38 mg chol., 97 mg sodium, 12 g carbo., 0 g fiber, 1 g pro.

Coconut Macadamia Pie

Cream of coconut and coconut milk are not the same. Coconut milk is pressed from the flesh of the coconut, while cream of coconut (used in piña coladas) is a thick, sweet liquid made from fresh coconuts.

PREP: 15 minutes
BAKE: at 450° about 10 minutes
COOK: about 18 minutes
CHILL: at least 5 hours or overnight
MAKES: 8 servings

1	refrigerated ready-to-roll piecrust
1	can (15 ounces) cream of coconut
2	boxes (3 ounces each) cook-and-serve vanilla pudding mix
1¾	cups milk
1	jar (4 ounces) macadamia nuts, coarsely chopped (about ¾ cup)
1½	cups heavy cream
⅔	cup sweet flake coconut, toasted

1. Heat oven to 450°. Place piecrust in 9-inch pie plate; crimp edges. Bake at 450° about 10 minutes or until golden. Cool completely on wire rack.

2. Reserve 3 tablespoons of the cream of coconut. In medium-size saucepan, mix remaining cream of coconut, pudding mix and milk. Cook over medium heat, stirring constantly, until mixture comes to full boil and is very thick, about 18 minutes. Take off heat and stir in half of macadamia nuts. Pour filling into cooled piecrust and refrigerate for 2 hours.

3. In large bowl, beat cream and reserved cream of coconut with an electric mixer on medium speed to stiff peaks. Spread over top of pie. Top with remaining nuts and toasted coconut. Refrigerate at least 3 hours or overnight.

Per serving: 701 cal., 57 g total fat (35 g sat.), 68 mg chol., 307 mg sodium, 45 g carbo., 3 g fiber, 7 g pro.

Black and White Brownies

You'd never guess that this "fancified" recipe, jazzed up with two kinds of chocolate chips, pecans and a decadent cocoa frosting, starts with a brownie mix.

PREP: 25 minutes
BAKE: at 350° about 31 minutes
COOL: 1½ hours
MAKES: 36 bars

Brownies:
- 1   box (19 to 21 ounces) fudge brownie mix
- 1   package (10 to 12 ounces) white baking chips
- 1   cup semisweet chocolate chips
- ½   cup pecan pieces

Frosting:
- 4   tablespoons (½ stick) butter, melted
- 3   tablespoons hot water
- 2   cups confectioners' sugar
- ¼   cup unsweetened cocoa powder
- 1   teaspoon vanilla extract
- ¾   cup pecan pieces

1. Brownies: Heat oven to 350°. Grease bottom of 13×9×2-inch baking pan. Prepare brownie mix following package directions. Stir in half of white baking chips, all of semisweet chocolate chips and the ½ cup pecans. Spread batter in pan.

2. Bake at 350° about 30 minutes or until center is set. Sprinkle with half of remaining white baking chips; return to oven for 1 minute. Cool on wire rack.

3. Frosting: In medium-size bowl, combine melted butter and hot water; stir in confectioners' sugar, cocoa powder and vanilla. Beat by hand until smooth; spoon over top of brownies. Sprinkle with the ¾ cup pecans and remaining white baking pieces. Cool 1½ hours or until frosting is set. Cut into bars.

Per bar: 221 cal., 12 g total fat (4 g sat.), 18 mg chol., 67 mg sodium, 25 g carbo., 1 g fiber, 2 g pro.

Menus

It's your turn to host a gathering for family and friends, and it's the perfect time to impress. For a variety of events throughout the year, there's a menu that's a just-right match.

Springtime Dinner
Pan-Seared Lamb Chops with Mint Salad (page 51)
Steamed asparagus
Whole grain rolls with butter
Sour Cream Lemon Pie (page 170)
Sparkling water or dry white wine

Tailgate Gathering
Grilled brat sandwiches
Pioneer Beans (page 88)
Macaroni salad
Deviled eggs
Oatmeal Chocolate Chip Cookies (page 172)
Beer or soda pop

Summer Afternoon Supper
Grilled Southwestern Salmon Salad (page 96)
French baguette slices with butter
Chocolate Zucchini Bars (page 176)
Margaritas or lemonade

Fireside Supper
Family-Style Chili and Dumplings (page 70)
Tossed green salad
Apple-Walnut Bake (page 182)
Milk

Saturday Picnic Lunch
Sticky Sloppy Barbecue Chicken (page 109)
Corn on the cob with butter
Potato salad
Black and White Brownies (page 185)
Iced tea or beer

Sunday Brunch
Vegetable Frittata (page 40)
Breakfast sausage or bacon
Crunchy Toffee Mini Muffins (page 32)
Fresh mixed berries with yogurt
Coffee and/or fruit juice

Celebration Breakfast
Caramel-Pecan French Toast (page 44)
Scrambled eggs
Baked ham slice
Trifle Fruit Salad (page 35)
Coffee and/or fruit juice

Holiday Open House
Glazed Ham Balls and Smokies (page 24)
Brie with sliced apples and pears
Tricolor Tapenade (page 25)
Gouda Pecan Poppers (page 27)
Assorted holiday cookies and/or miniature desserts
Holiday Honey Punch (page 15)

Recipe Index

Note: Page numbers in **bold** refer to photographs.

Index

Index

Metric Information

The charts on this page provide a guide for converting measurements from the U.S. customary system, which is used throughout this book, to the metric system.

Product Differences

Most of the ingredients called for in the recipes in this book are available in most countries. However, some are known by different names. Here are some common American ingredients and their possible counterparts:

• Sugar (white) is granulated, fine granulated, or castor sugar.
• Powdered sugar is icing sugar.
• All-purpose flour is enriched, bleached or unbleached white household flour. When self-rising flour is used in place of all-purpose flour in a recipe that calls for leavening, omit the leavening agent (baking soda and baking powder) and salt.
• Light-colored corn syrup is golden syrup.
• Cornstarch is cornflour.
• Baking soda is bicarbonate of soda.
• Vanilla or vanilla extract is vanilla essence.
• Green, red, or yellow sweet peppers are capsicums or bell peppers.
• Golden raisins are sultanas.

Volume and Weight

The United States traditionally uses cup measures for liquid and solid ingredients. The chart below shows the approximate imperial and metric equivalents. If you are accustomed to weighing solid ingredients, the following approximate equivalents will be helpful.

• 1 cup butter, castor sugar, or rice = 8 ounces = ½ pound = 250 grams
• 1 cup flour = 4 ounces = ¼ pound = 125 grams
• 1 cup icing sugar = 5 ounces = 150 grams
• Canadian and U.S. volume for a cup measure is 8 fluid ounces (237 ml), but the standard metric equivalent is 250 ml.
• 1 British imperial cup is 10 fluid ounces.
• In Australia, 1 tablespoon equals 20 ml, and there are 4 teaspoons in the Australian tablespoon.
• Spoon measures are used for smaller amounts of ingredients. Although the size of the tablespoon varies slightly in different countries, for practical purposes and for recipes in this book, a straight substitution is all that's necessary. Measurements made using cups or spoons always should be level unless stated otherwise.

Common Weight Range Replacements

Imperial / U.S.	Metric
½ ounce	15 g
1 ounce	25 g or 30 g
4 ounces (¼ pound)	115 g or 125 g
8 ounces (½ pound)	225 g or 250 g
16 ounces (1 pound)	450 g or 500 g
1¼ pounds	625 g
1½ pounds	750 g
2 pounds or 2¼ pounds	1,000 g or 1 Kg

Oven Temperature Equivalents

Fahrenheit Setting		Gas Setting
300°F	150°C	Gas Mark 2 (very low)
325°F	160°C	Gas Mark 3 (low)
350°F	180°C	Gas Mark 4 (moderate)
375°F	190°C	Gas Mark 5 (moderate)
400°F	200°C	Gas Mark 6 (hot)
425°F	220°C	Gas Mark 7 (hot)
450°F	230°C	Gas Mark 8 (very hot)
475°F	240°C	Gas Mark 9 (very hot)
500°F	260°C	Gas Mark 10 (extremely hot)
Broil	Broil	Grill

*Electric and gas ovens may be calibrated using celsius. However, for an electric oven, increase celsius setting 10 to 20 degrees when cooking above 160°C. For convection or forced air ovens (gas or electric), lower the temperature setting 25°F/10°C when cooking at all heat levels.

Baking Pan Sizes

Imperial / U.S.	Metric
9×1½-inch round cake pan	22- or 23×4-cm (1.5 L)
9×1½-inch pie plate	22- or 23×4-cm (1 L)
8×8×2-inch square cake pan	20×5-cm (2 L)
9×9×2-inch square cake pan	22- or 23×4.5-cm (2.5 L)
11×7×1½-inch baking pan	28×17×4-cm (2 L)
2-quart rectangular baking pan	30×19×4.5-cm (3 L)
13×9×2-inch baking pan	34×22×4.5-cm (3.5 L)
15×10×1-inch jelly roll pan	40×25×2-cm
9×5×3-inch loaf pan	23×13×8-cm (2 L)
2-quart casserole	2 L

U.S. / Standard Metric Equivalents

⅛ teaspoon = 0.5 ml	
¼ teaspoon = 1 ml	
½ teaspoon = 2 ml	
1 teaspoon = 5 ml	
1 tablespoon = 15 ml	
2 tablespoons = 25 ml	
¼ cup = 2 fluid ounces = 50 ml	
⅓ cup = 3 fluid ounces = 75 ml	
½ cup = 4 fluid ounces = 125 ml	
⅔ cup = 5 fluid ounces = 150 ml	
¾ cup = 6 fluid ounces = 175 ml	
1 cup = 8 fluid ounces = 250 ml	
2 cups = 1 pint = 500 ml	
1 quart = 1 litre	